THE CIVIL WAR

JULIUS CAESAR

TRANSLATED BY THE REV. F. P. LONG, M.A.
SOMETIME EXHIBITIONER OF WORCESTER
COLLEGE

INTRODUCTION BY JONATHAN PRAG

BARNES
———
NEW Y

THE BARNES & NOBLE
LIBRARY OF ESSENTIAL READING

Introduction and Suggested Reading
© 2005 by Barnes & Noble, Inc.

Originally published circa 44 BCE

This 2005 edition published by Barnes & Noble, Inc.

Barnes & Noble, Inc.
122 Fifth Avenue
New York, NY 10011

ISBN-13: 978-0-7607-6894-5
ISBN-10: 0-7607-6894-3

Printed and bound in the United States of America

7 9 10 8 6

CONTENTS

BOOK III
DYRRACHIUM AND PHARSALIA

LIST OF MAPS

INTRODUCTION

THE CIVIL WAR IS JULIUS CAESAR'S PERSONAL ACCOUNT OF HIS WAR
with Pompey the Great—the war which destroyed the five-hundred-
year-old Roman Republic. Caesar the victor became Caesar the
dictator, who was assassinated by Brutus on the Ides of March, 44 BC.
From the ruin of the Republic arose Caesar's adopted son, Octavian,
later Augustus, the first Roman Emperor. The crossing of the Rubicon by Caesar, in January 49 BC, is, quite simply, one of the most
symbolic moments in world history. In three short books, Caesar
describes how, in order to defend his *dignitas* (honor), and the *libertas*
(freedom) of both himself and the Roman people, he marched on
Rome, and defeated the forces of Pompey and the Senate in Italy,
Spain, and Greece. Caesar's "commentaries," written in famously
simple prose, with the distinctive use of the third person, offer a
unique opportunity to read the victor's version of events, written by
one of the greatest figures in world history, the first "Caesar."

Caius Julius Caesar was born on 13 July 100 BC. His family, the
Julii, claimed descent from the ancient kings of Rome, and from
the goddess Venus (through her son Aeneas). Caesar was the nephew
of the general Caius Marius, and in his youth he witnessed the
rise of the military warlords of the last years of the Roman Republic,
Marius, Sulla, Crassus, and Pompey. He rapidly carved out an impres-
sive political career of his own, forging an alliance with Pompey and

Crassus in 60 BC. This won for him a military command in Gaul (southern France), and in ten years of spectacular campaigns he extended Roman rule to the Rhine and the Atlantic—and mounted the first Roman invasion of Britain. But competition for honors with his contemporary Pompey the Great, and the political maneuvers of other fellow senators, placed Caesar in what he saw as an untenable position. At the start of 49 BC, faced with the choice between political extinction and civil war, Caesar gambled on war and led a single legion of his Gallic veterans across the River Rubicon (which marked the northern boundary of "Italy"). The die was cast. The tradition that has built up around Caesar is immense and ambiguous. The reader will not find Caesar's famous quote in his writings—"I came, I saw, I conquered," after Zela, in Cilicia, in 47 BC. Although seemingly unfinished and unpublished at his death, *The Civil War* is instead his own attempt at an explanation of the war that changed the Roman world, a version summed up by the words placed in his mouth by one ancient biographer, Suetonius, *hoc voluerunt*, "they asked for it!"

For all its apparent simplicity, *The Civil War* is not an easy work to understand, nor is Caesar an easy man to assess. The death of the regent of Egypt in late 48 BC, and not the death of Pompey (28 September 48 BC), marks the end of book 3, and this is not an obvious point of closure. The Civil Wars, for Caesar, dragged on until the Battle of Munda in Spain in 45 BC. The account, as we have it, seems to have been published after Caesar's death, in 44 BC, by one of his officers, Aulus Hirtius, or so Hirtius himself tells us in the eighth and final book of Caesar's earlier commentaries on his Gallic Wars (covering 58–50 BC). Hirtius completed Caesar's *The Conquest of Gaul* by writing book 8 (52–50 BC), published Caesar's three books on the Civil War (49–48 BC), and then either he or another wrote the surviving commentaries on the Egyptian, African, and Spanish phases of the Civil Wars (48–45 BC). It is commonly accepted today that Caesar therefore wrote what we have as *The Civil War* no later than the winter of 48–47 BC, when he was held up in Alexandria (with Cleopatra); but that the events which followed, both in Egypt and Rome, culminating in his adoption of the position of Dictator for Life, rendered publication pointless in his eyes. In other words, his claims (especially at I.7 and 22) to be defending both his *dignitas* and the freedom of himself and others from the oppression of a *factio paucorum* (the faction of a few) rang increasingly hollow in his own ears as much as those of others, the more distant became the likelihood of a return to Republican normality.

Such a view requires brief consideration of the genre in which Caesar was writing and his reasons for writing. But to consider these things in turn demands that we examine the context for the Civil War itself. Throughout, the opinions of both contemporaries and later writers overshadow what can be said. When studying the ancient world, the evidence is always less than we would wish; it is particularly rich, comparatively speaking, for this moment in time, but nonetheless, it is highly partial. We have letters to and from the contemporary orator and statesman Marcus Tullius Cicero, who struggled in vain to compose the strife; we have the writings of, and attributed to, the contemporary historian Sallust; we have the anti-Caesarian verse account of the Civil War by the Neronian poet Lucan (also known as the *Pharsalia*); we have the biographies of Caesar written by Plutarch and Suetonius, ca. 150 years after his death; and we have the historical accounts of Appian's *Civil Wars* and Cassius Dio's *Roman History*, written in the second and third centuries AD respectively. On the other hand, we do not have the contemporary history of Asinius Pollio, though it clearly underlies much of what does survive in other writers.

The writing of commentaries on campaigns was by no means a novel practice. It belonged to an age in which the writing of history, understood as the history of men, politics, and action, was commonplace, and had been ever since Thucydides had set forth his version of the Peloponnesian War between Athens and Sparta, in which he had fought. However, commentaries in general were intended as notes for a proper literary history, not as a finished product by themselves. Caesar had already broken the mold with his *The Conquest of Gaul*, of which Cicero wrote, in 46 BC:

They are like nude figures, straight and beautiful; stripped of all ornament of style as if they had laid aside a garment. His aim was to furnish others with material for writing history, and perhaps he has succeeded in gratifying the inept, who may wish to apply their curling irons to his material; but men of sound judgment he has deterred from writing, since in history there is nothing more pleasing than brevity, clear and correct.

We know that Caesar sent back reports to the Senate and People of Rome on a regular basis. *The Conquest of Gaul* is however something grander, even if still written up a year at a time, in the leisure of the winters between campaigns. These books belong in a culture in which the *gloria* won through military achievements was all-important, and its emphasis all the more necessary during a prolonged absence from Rome. We must assume the same thing for *The Civil War.* A shift in style has been suggested between the first two books, covering the year 49 BC, and the third, covering 48 BC. This would fit with annual composition.

Cicero's praise was written under Caesar the dictator. By contrast, Asinius Pollio, writing shortly after Caesar's death, thought the commentaries to have been written rather carelessly and with too little regard for the whole truth. The speed of composition and the probable lack of revision by Caesar himself might partly defend Caesar from such an accusation. Scholars have often sought to control Caesar's account, and although it is true that there are omissions (e.g., a mutiny by his legions, which belongs at II.22.6, but is reported only in later accounts such as Suetonius, *Divus Iulius* 69), disparities (compare Caesar's report of the negotiations attempted through N. Magius at Brindisium in I.24.4 and 26.2, with the letter of Caesar preserved among Cicero's *Letters to Atticus,* IX.13.a), and distortions (the chronological sequence of events in the opening phase of the war is not that implied by Caesar's account), it would be hard to accuse Caesar of gross falsehood. J. P. V. D. Balsdon concluded that "Caesar could not claim to have written 'the truth, the whole truth and nothing but the truth.'" But the value of this lies, as Leo Raditsa observed, precisely in the fact that "As often in first-rate ancient historians, Caesar desires his reader to think what he does not state outright." And to glimpse the mind of Caesar is a precious thing. The real problem, as so often, is that we lack sufficient contemporary evidence always to control Caesar's account.

However, the Gallic commentaries were written to bring home Caesar's achievements on behalf of the Roman state to the Roman people (or at least the upper echelons of the Roman people). As a motive—and genre—this sits very uncomfortably with a civil war fought against other members of the Roman senate. The exact reasons why Caesar should both have begun, and then abandoned, the attempt to write an account of his actions in a civil war will always remain obscure, but we can speculate. However, to do so we must consider the context and nature of the civil war.

"Caesar would tolerate no superior, Pompey no equal." Such was the judgment of antiquity, and it deserves our notice. The Roman Republic was not a democracy (whatever the views expressed in the translator's introduction, on which see below). At its heart was a largely closed ruling elite. Members of this elite competed for office, and in particular the highest office, the consulate, to which two men were elected annually. Election was by the people, but the people were constituted in a fashion which favored the wealthy, and voting was heavily influenced by political loyalties and alliances, by social bonds such as clientship, and by the use of wealth (which might be crudely, if not entirely accurately, classified as bribery). It is an unavoidable fact that the majority of those elected to the consulate came from families that had already achieved the consulate in the past. For this elite, one's *dignitas* (honor) and *auctoritas* ("non-executive "power," or "influence") derived from the winning of honors such as the consulate, which lay in the gift of the Roman people and conferred *gloria*. Success in war had long been the most traditional means to the winning of such honors, and from this derived much of the Roman Republic's imperial success.

The success of the Republic in turn depended on the self-regulation by this elite of its internal competition. No one member could dominate—he could do so only at the expense of his fellows, who could be expected to restrain him. The system, in principle, had enough honors to go round. In the later part of the Roman Republic, and especially in the period of Caesar's lifetime, this structure began to break down. The political machinery was that of a city-state, not a Mediterranean empire, and the expansion of empire led to an increase in the number of lesser magistracies, but not to a systematic revision of the constitution. Consequently, a growing number of men came to compete for the consulship, of which there were still only ever two per year. The growth of empire likewise meant that the rewards to be had from the consulship became ever greater. The system became further imbalanced with the increase in special, one-off commands to deal with specific problems, such as piracy, the corn-supply of Rome, or particular wars. Added to this, the Republic never developed a state-run, professional army, but rather, troops, employed on increasingly distant, long-term campaigns, became dependent upon the beneficence of their commanding officer, or some other politician, to finance their demobilization. In combination, this situation encouraged the rise of highly ambitious individuals, supported by veteran armies of soldiers trained on extended campaigns and who looked to their commander to provide for their futures. Such individuals, born to compete with their peers for honors, found themselves in situations where the normal restraints suddenly lacked any relevance. As Lucius Cornelius Sulla had starkly demonstrated, first in 87 BC and then again in 82 BC, all one had to do was march at the head of one's army to Rome and demand one's due. Those who resisted could be swept aside. But as R. Syme observed, "the true glory of a Roman aristocrat [was] to contend with his peers for primacy, not to destroy them," and Caesar's defense of his *dignitas* was ultimately his undoing.

This is of course a gross simplification, but it will aid analysis. By the end of the 50s BC, Caesar and especially Pompey had both held several extended commands, far beyond anything their predecessors or contemporaries could expect, or even match. Caesar had been consul in 59 BC, and proceeded from that to a hugely successful campaign of conquest in France, Belgium, and Germany, which by any normal expectation would have earned him quite spectacular honors and recognition on his return to Rome. Pompey, on the other hand, had achieved similar successes in the eastern Mediterranean in the 60s BC, and now held special commands for the control of Spain and the maintenance of the corn supply. He had won the consulship very early, back in 70 BC, and twice more in 55 and 52 BC. Caesar now aimed for the consulship again, an honor which he felt his due, but also one which he perhaps saw as necessary in order to maintain the position he had reached. Without it, further great commands would be difficult, but he would also find it hard to resist the attacks that were likely to come from other senators for his actions, not all of them entirely legal, over the preceding fifteen years.

Since 60 BC, Caesar and Pompey had been in uneasy alliance, for their mutual advancement (together with Marcus Crassus, who died in 53 BC). Since antiquity, this unofficial triumvirate has often been seen (by Pollio, Horace, Lucan, and others) as the real start of the Civil War. The remainder of the Senate was still sufficiently powerful to resist the demands of figures such as Pompey and Caesar, and a small group of conservatives, under the leadership of a senator called Marcus Porcius Cato, had in general sought to resist such abnormal grants of honors. It was their opposition which had inspired the triumvirate in the first place. Conservative (*optimates* in Latin) is something of a misnomer, since the senatorial oligarchy, by its very nature, was conservative; the difference lay rather in the methods used to win *dignitas*, *gloria*, and *auctoritas*, either traditional or more popular (the *populares*); there was essentially no difference of opinion about the overall system. This group now sought to split apart the coalition of Pompey and Caesar, to bring Pompey within its number, and thereby to resist Caesar's claims all the more successfully. It was the resistance of this group to the idea that Caesar should receive preferential treatment in his pursuit of a second consulship (in particular the right to stand *in absentia*, while still holding his Gallic command) which directly caused the Civil War. That is, of course, not the same thing as to say that it was their fault (although some, both in antiquity and today, would lay the blame at Cato's door—including Caesar, who claimed to resist the unjust "faction of a few" of Cato and his allies).

It was only in the very last months of 50 BC that contemporaries actually began to speak of the possibility of civil war (as for instance Marcus Caelius Rufus, in a letter to Cicero, written in August 50 BC). The historian struggles with hindsight at such a moment. In the eyes of some, such as E. S. Gruen, there was no significant break between Pompey and Caesar before this time (in the view of others, events such as the death of Crassus in 53 BC mark the point of no return). But it is not simply a question of when war became inevitable. If *The Civil War* is Caesar's account of his actions, its very existence requires that we ask why Caesar went to war; and that impels us to ask whether Caesar intended war and, if so, from what moment. Christian Meier, in one of the most important later twentieth-century interpretations of Caesar's life, has suggested that the reason Caesar could contemplate civil war was because he was able to view the political system and the situation from outside. The father of modern Roman history, Theodor Mommsen, held the view that Caesar planned an overthrow of the senate from an early date, and that his Gallic campaigns were but the staging ground for the march on Rome. But such views perhaps fall victim to the perennial fascination which great figures in history hold. Matthias Gelzer, author of the fundamental modern biography of Caesar, did not doubt Caesar's greatness as a statesman, but remained ultimately agnostic on his vision and motives. Where Caesar differed from his contemporaries was in his speed of decision, and in his level of determination to carry through his will to completed action. Not for nothing was Caesar the general famed for his *celeritas* (swiftness), and throughout *The Civil War*, just as in *The Conquest of Gaul*, one sees Caesar again and again transforming a seemingly weak position by his remarkable ability to thrust his opponent onto the defensive.

It is the very existence of *The Civil War* that gives the lie to the view that Caesar long planned the Republic's fall. Just as Cicero's own manifesto for the Roman Republic (the *De Re Publica*, "On the Republic"), written in 54 BC, did not involve any radical transformation of the system, neither did Caesar's attack constitute a revolution. Believing Caesar to be just one step along the way to transforming the Republic into an empire, Ronald Syme claimed, "Caesar was not a revolutionary," in his classic *The Roman Revolution*. Contrast the actions of Marcus Caelius Rufus, an ambitious and youthful supporter of Caesar's, whose misguided attempt to stir up the underclasses and debtors of Italy led to his death and was in no way supported by Caesar (described briefly in III.20–22). Caesar instead claimed the support of all Italy and seems to have been the preferred choice of the Italian propertied classes and in particular of creditors. The *libertas*, "freedom," which he saw to be oppressed by his opponents was the freedom of a senator to compete for the honors of the Roman people, honors which he believed that he had more than warranted in his ten years of campaigning, and for which Pompey's career offered plentiful precedents. To yield would be to lose all that he had so far won, and with it his *dignitas*. When Pompey sought the protection of his own *dignitas* by claiming to defend the position of the Senate (and so the future support of this group in his own maintenance of position), Pompey denied Caesar, in Caesar's view, what was rightfully his.

What *The Civil War* so bluntly demonstrates, in the language of Caesar's speech to his troops in I.7, or his exchange with Lentulus Spinther at Corfinium (I.22), is that Caesar saw all this in terms of the Republic. He could hardly do otherwise. What the non-publication of *The Civil War* suggests is that the Republic was rendered obsolete by the Civil War and Caesar's subsequent attempts to control the system, and a defense in those terms became an irrelevancy. Caesar's ability to comprehend that transformation does not mean that it was the reason that led Caesar to war in the first place. That is the benefit of hindsight, which has plagued the assessment of Caesar from the moment his gamble came off. Lucan (*The Civil War* I.670–72), writing under the Emperor Nero, a century later, concluded bitterly that "During the civil wars, every party and every leader professed to be defending the cause of liberty and of peace. Those ideals were incompatible. When peace came, it was the peace of despotism."

It remains for the reader to reach his own conclusions about one of the great conflicts in history. Caesar's account contains little about the crossing of the Rubicon, in contrast to later versions. This may, quite plausibly, be because at the time it did not appear to have the significance that later events came to give it. The account of Caesar has the great merit of being the principal protagonist's contemporary account of his actions. But just as he therefore has one particular view, which his non-publication may be taken to suggest changed with time, so Lucan, living with the consequences of his action, a century later had a rather different interpretation. The attitudes expressed in the translator's introduction further demonstrate that any assessment is inextricably linked with its historical moment. Long's introduction deserves reading, for it is no less instructive. But the parallels claimed with the British Empire are naturally intended to cast as positive a light on British rule as they are upon Caesar. Few would today agree with an assessment of the Roman Republic that classified it as "the freest of democratic institutions." Few too would care to be associated with an account which spoke of the "administration of backward races." But such a critique should give us pause for thought, before we jump too soon to our own interpretations of a different time and place.

Jonathan Prag is a lecturer in ancient history at the University of Leicester (UK). He has written a prize-winning doctoral thesis on Sicily under the Roman Republic, and he specializes in Republican history and the study of Greek and Latin epigraphy.

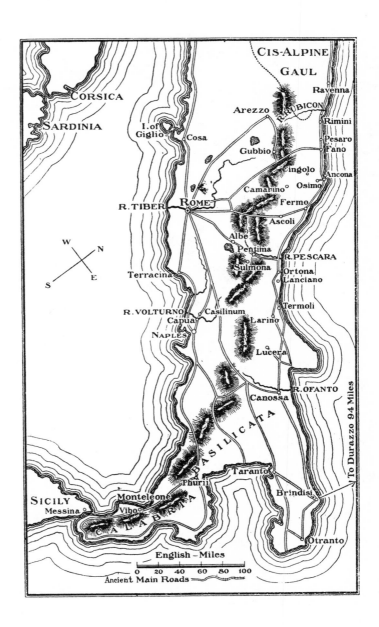

CIS-ALPINE
GAUL

CORSICA
SARDINIA

Ravenna
Arezzo
RUBICON
Rimini
I. of
Giglio
Cosa
Pesaro
Fano
Gubbio
Cingolo
Ancona
Camarino
Osimo
R.TIBER
ROME
Fermo
Ascoli
Albe
Pentima
R.PESCARA
Sulmona
Ortona
Terracina
Lanciano

R.VOLTURNO
Casilinum
Termoli
Capua
Larino
NAPLES
Lucera

R.OFANTO
Canossa

BASILICATA

Taranto

SICILY
Messina
Monteleone
Thurii
Brindisi
Vibo

CALABRIA
Otranto

To Durazzo 94 Miles

English — Miles

0   20   40   60   80   100

Ancient Main Roads

BOOK I

ITALY AND SPAIN

→ CHAPTER ONE ←

THE OUTBREAK OF WAR

WHEN CAESAR'S DISPATCH REACHED THE CONSULS, IT WAS ONLY THE urgent representations of the tribunes that gained it a hearing by the House; the further request for a definite motion on its terms was refused, and the House passed, at the instance of the Government, to the general debate upon public affairs. Lucius Lentulus pledged his support to the Senate and Republic, provided members were ready to express themselves with boldness and determination; but any coquetting with Caesar or bidding for his favor, such as they had shown in previous years, would find him consulting his own interests without the slightest heed to their decrees. "He, as well as they," he added significantly, "had his line of retreat open to him in the favor and friendship of Caesar." Scipio[2] spoke in similar terms. Pompeius was resolved to stand by the Republic if supported by the Senate; but let them hesitate or shrink from decided measures, and any subsequent appeal to his aid, should they afterwards desire it, would only be made in vain. This speech of Scipio's was taken by the House as representing the actual language of Pompeius; for, although they were met within the city walls, Pompeius was at the time in the neighborhood of Rome.[3] Other and more conciliatory measures, it should be noticed, had been previously counselled by various members present. Marcus Marcellus, for example, in addressing the House had urged that it was premature to discuss the main issue till levies had been completed throughout Italy, and armies put into commission; under whose protection they could then venture to formulate their wishes with liberty and security. Again, Marcus Calidius had a proposal that Pompeius should leave Italy and go off to his provinces,[4] thereby removing all pretext for war; since what Caesar feared was that the retention near the capital of the two legions lately extorted from him by the Senate should look like a deliberate menace from Pompeius to himself. This proposal of Calidius was repeated, with slight verbal changes, by Marcus Caelius Rufus.

They were one and all made the object of a savage attack by the presiding consul Lentulus, and effectually silenced by his scathing satire: in fact, he even went so far as to refuse to put the motion of Calidius; whereupon Marcellus, alarmed at the growing storm of obloquy, withdrew that standing in his name. The result was that this language of the consul, backed up by the terrorizing effect of the presence of the army, together with the open threats of Pompeius' friends, succeeded in forcing the House, against the convictions of the majority, to adopt the motion of Scipio, whereby Caesar was to disband his army before a fixed date or be held guilty of open treason. This resolution being vetoed by two of the tribunes, Marcus Antonius and Quintus Cassius, the legality of such veto was immediately challenged.[5] Extreme opinions were expressed, and the applause that greeted each speaker from the ranks of Caesar's opponents was in direct proportion to the bitter and vindictive spirit each displayed.

It was evening before the Senate broke up, and Pompeius at once summoned to a conference outside the city all who, possessed a seat in the House, praising their recent action and stiffening them to face the future, while rebuking and stimulating the faint-hearted. From all parts of the country large numbers of those who had belonged to the old Pompeian armies were called out for active service, induced by hopes of plunder and high military rank; many also of those who were attached to the two legions lately transferred by Caesar now received orders to be in attendance; with the result that the city, the ascent to the Capitol, and the Comitium were soon crowded with regimental officers, centurions, and reservists. An overflowing meeting of the House was shortly afterwards held, packed with the friends of both consuls, and the supporters, not merely of Pompeius, but of all who nursed old grievances against Caesar; and these, by their threatening language and imposing numbers, intimidated the weak-kneed, strengthened the waverers, and made a free decision for most of those present impossible. An offer was made by Lucius Piso, one of the censors,[6] and Lucius Roscius, one of the praetors,[7] to carry a report of these proceedings to Caesar, six days only being asked for the purpose: similarly others urged that a commission be sent to lay before him the mind of the House.

To all alike objection was raised, and all alike were thwarted by speeches from the consul, from Scipio, and from Cato. Cato's opposition was due to long-standing dislike of Caesar, increased by resentment at an electoral defeat. The action of the consul Lentulus was dictated by the colossal proportions of his debts, which he looked forward to settling by the command of an army and provinces, and by the princely profits to be made out of foreign king-making: indeed, he boasted in private that he would be a second Sulla, into whose hands the supreme government would one day fall. As for Scipio, his motives were similar ambitions for a province and armies, the command of which he thought he, as a relative, would share with Pompeius: to this must be added his fears of prosecution, and also the ostentatious flattery of which he was at this time the subject, not merely from himself, but from all his most powerful contemporaries in the political and legal worlds. Finally, in the case of Pompeius, the influence of Caesar's opponents along with his inability to tolerate a rival on equal terms, had induced him completely to withdraw his old friendship and to resume intimate relations with their common antagonists, whose enmity, in the majority of cases, he had himself fastened upon Caesar in the old days of their family alliance.[8] In addition to this, the public stigma attaching to the affair of the two legions, which, instead of marching for Asia Minor and Syria, had been diverted by him to secure his own sovereignty, drove him to work for a settlement by the sword.

It was such considerations that now caused everything to be hurried through in disorder. The delay asked for by Caesar's friends, in order to acquaint him with these developments, was steadily refused; the two tribunes of the people were allowed no opportunity either of protesting against their personal peril, or even of maintaining, in the form of the veto, that fundamental right of their office which had been left them by Lucius Sulla. The seventh day of the New Year saw them compelled to take measures for their personal safety, such as, in the case of the notorious revolutionaries of the past, had generally been adopted as their hazardous refuge only after eight months spent in multifarious political activity. Such indecent haste, in fact, was now displayed, that without more ado recourse was had to the very last weapon of Senatorial government, the well-known "final decree," which no amount of effrontery in popular legislators had ever before brought to a division in the House, unless indeed Rome were all but burning, and the very existence of the country despaired of, the decree directing consuls, praetors, tribunes, and all proconsuls near the capital to take measures for the safety of the State. This order was embodied in a decree of the House dated January 7: and thus within the first five days on which the Senate could legally be convened since Lentulus entered upon office (not reckoning the two days set down for comitial business), a decision was arrived at of extreme severity and malignity both on the question of Caesar's military command, and on the fate of two distinguished tribunes of the people. The latter at once left Rome and fled to Caesar, who was then at Ravenna, awaiting an answer to his very moderate demands, and still hoping that men's general sense of fairness would render a peaceful solution possible.

The next few days the Senate met outside the city boundary. The conduct of Pompeius tallied with the forecast given of it by Scipio. After commending the courage and firmness that the Senators had just displayed, he proceeded to lay before them an account of the military forces at his disposal, which were not less, he declared, than ten fully mobilized Roman legions. To this was added the statement that he had trustworthy intelligence that Caesar's troops looked coldly on his schemes, and could neither be induced to support his cause, nor to follow his leadership. Motions were then put before the House dealing with other requisite measures. It was proposed that enlisting should be organized throughout Italy; that Faustus Sulla should be dispatched without delay to Morocco (*Mauretania*); and lastly, that Pompeius should be supplied with money from the Treasury. The question was also raised of making an alliance of friendship with King Juba,[9] but the consul Marcellus refused for the present to entertain this idea; whilst the proposal concerning Faustus was vetoed by Philippus, one of the tribunes. The rest were duly embodied in regular decrees. It was further determined to give commands of provinces to men not then in office, two of these to be consular and the rest praetorian. Of the former Syria fell to Scipio, Gaul to Lucius Domitius. By a clandestine arrangement Philippus and Cotta were passed over, neither of their lots being thrown in. To the remaining provinces ex-praetors were sent out; and these, without waiting for the legal confirmation of their command by the people, after offering the customary state-prayers, immediately left the capital in full military attire. The consuls, acting against all precedent, took their departure from the city, whilst inside and on the Capitol lictors were seen in attendance on men no longer in office, a sight unexampled in the history of the commonwealth. Over the whole of Italy troops were being enlisted, arms commandeered, money levied on the country towns and even plundered from the temples; in short, every distinction between the claims of the State and of religion was obliterated.

Caesar no sooner had intelligence of these proceedings than he appealed to his troops. After recounting in detail the wrongs he had suffered at the hands of his political opponents, he charged Pompeius with having allowed his mind to be misled, and his judgment to be warped by the pernicious influence these exerted upon him, owing to the petty jealousy he felt at his rival's reputation; and that, despite the fact that that rival had himself always actively supported the power and prestige of Pompeius. A further grievance was the establishment of an unwarrantable precedent in the constitution, when military force was invoked to annul and to override the tribunes' power of veto—that same veto which in past years had only been restored by a similar appeal to force. Even Sulla, who stripped the tribunician office of all its functions, yet left it the free exercise of the veto; Pompeius, who was regarded as the restorer of their lost privileges, had actually succeeded in robbing them of what they had always enjoyed. Again, on every occasion when the well-known decree had been passed for the magistrates "to see to it that the country take no harm"—the statutory formula for summoning the Roman people to arms—it had been at a time either of the promulgation of some obnoxious legislation, of some violence offered by a tribune, or of some popular disturbance; and then only after the temples and city heights had already been seized. How such revolutionary attempts in past history had been avenged by the downfall of Saturninus and the Gracchi, he next reminded them. Yet of these circumstances not one had at this time arisen or been even thought of: no law had been promulgated, no popular legislation proposed, no disturbance taken place. He called upon them now to protect from political adversaries the honor and good name of their commander, under whose leadership for nine long years they had fought with such brilliant success the battles of their country, during which time they had gained such numberless victories, and subjugated the whole of Gaul and Germany.[10]

The men of the Thirteenth legion, the only one present, answered with a cheer (Caesar had summoned this regiment to him when the general levy in Italy began; the concentration of the others was not yet completed), "they were ready to protect the rights of their commander and of the people's tribunes."

Assured of the temper of his troops, Caesar began his advance with this legion as far as Rimini (*Ariminum*),[11] where he met the two tribunes who had lately fled to his protection: his remaining legions he ordered out of their winter quarters with instructions to follow close in his rear. At Rimini he was waited on by young Lucius Caesar, a son of one of his own generals. This young man, after first stating the primary object of his mission, went on to explain that he had a private message from Pompeius to Caesar on the subject of their personal relations. This was to the effect that "Pompeius desired to clear himself in Caesar's eyes, so that the latter should not take as an insult to himself what had solely been dictated by public exigencies; that he had always regarded the claims of public interests as prior to those of private friendship, and that Caesar similarly should now show his true greatness by sacrificing ambition and passion to the general good, and not allow resentment against opponents to go so far as to involve his country in the punishment he hoped to inflict upon them." There was more in the same strain along with excuses for the conduct of Pompeius; and a very similar appeal, in similar language, was made to Caesar by the praetor Roscius, who stated that he had it from Pompeius.

Now, although this episode had apparently but little bearing on the removal of his own grievances, yet, finding appropriate agents at hand for conveying his wishes to Pompeius, Caesar begged each of them that, as they had brought him Pompeius' terms, so they would not object to taking back his own demands to Pompeius. It was surely worthwhile to go to a little trouble, if by this means a great quarrel could be settled and the whole of Italy thus freed from apprehension.

Let them then understand that with him honor had always been first, dearer than life itself. This honor had been wounded when the privilege granted him by the people of Rome had been floutingly snatched from him by opponents, and when, after being robbed of six months' command, he found himself, as he now did, dragged back to the capital, in spite of the fact that a resolution allowing his candidature at the approaching elections to be accepted in his absence had been expressly passed by the sovereign people.[12] Though, however, he had borne without complaint, for the sake of public peace, this curtailment of his rights, yet his own modest suggestion for a general disarmament, which he made in a dispatch to the Senate, had been bluntly refused: levies were even now proceeding throughout Italy; whilst the two legions which had been detached from his command on the pretext of a Parthian war, were still detained at home: in short, the whole country was in arms. What did all this point to except his own destruction? Still, he was ready to stoop to every humiliation and to endure every injustice, if thereby he could save the commonwealth. Accordingly, these were his terms: Pompeius to take his departure to his own provinces, and both to disband their armies simultaneously with a general disarmament in Italy. That would allay the apprehension of the country, and enable elections and the whole machinery of government to be carried on by both Senate and people without coercion. Lastly, in order to facilitate the settlement by giving it fixed terms and the sanction of their sworn oath, he proposed that either Pompeius should advance to meet him, or else allow a visit from himself; for he felt confident that by talking matters over all differences could be adjusted.

With this message Roscius and Lucius Caesar came to Capua, where they found the consuls and Pompeius, to whom they delivered Caesar's stipulations. After due deliberation an answer was returned by the same messengers, who thereupon brought back the written demands the other side had to make, of which the following represents the summary: "Caesar must recross the Rubicon, evacuate Rimini, and disband his army; after that, Pompeius would go to his Spanish provinces. Meanwhile, until a pledge had been given that Caesar would keep his word, the consuls and Pompeius would continue to raise troops."

It was obviously a one-sided bargain to require Caesar to evacuate Rimini and retire upon his province, whilst his opponent kept both provinces and legions alike to which he had no claim: to propose that Caesar's army should be disbanded, while yet proceeding with his own levy: or again, to undertake to go to his province, without, however, fixing a date for his departure. The consequence of this last provision would have been that, supposing at the close of Caesar's consulship Pompeius had not yet left Rome, he could not justly be held guilty of any breach of faith by this refusal to quit the capital. Finally, his omission to arrange an interview or to promise any visit could but reduce the chances of peace to a minimum. Accordingly Caesar dispatched Marcus Antonius with a force of five battalions to seize Arrezo (*Arretium*), whilst he himself remained with two more at Rimini, where the raising of fresh troops was forthwith commenced. At the same time, with the three remaining battalions of his single legion he occupied the coast towns of Pesaro (*Pisaurum*), Fano (*Fanum*), and Ancona.

During these same few days intelligence reached him that the praetor Thermus, with a force of five battalions was at Gubbio (*Iguvium*), engaged in fortifying the town, the inhabitants of which were all strongly disposed towards himself. Under the command therefore of Curio the three battalions stationed at Pesaro and Rimini were at once ordered to the place. On hearing of their approach Thermus, who felt no confidence in the temper of the town, hastily withdrew his garrison; but his men deserted on the march to return to their homes, and Curio was then left to receive an enthusiastic reception into Gubbio.

The report of these proceedings determined Caesar to trust the adhesion of the country boroughs, and, by withdrawing the battalions of the Thirteenth legion then garrisoning them, to march upon Osimo (*Auximum*). This town was then held by Attius, who, after throwing a few battalions into it as a garrison, was now engaged in raising troops throughout the whole of Piceno (*Picenum*) with the help of a number of senators who were traversing the country for that purpose.

On the news of Caesar's advance, however, the town councilors of Osimo waited in a body upon Attius Varus, and informed him that, without constituting themselves judges in the present quarrel, neither they nor the rest of the town were prepared to see a general like Caius Caesar, whose public services had been so signal, refused admission within their walls; and that he would therefore do well to consult his future interests. This language led Varus to make a precipitate withdrawal of the garrison he had established in the town; but, overtaken by a small knot of infantry from Caesar's advanced companies and compelled to give battle, he found himself deserted by his troops, who either dispersed to their homes or went over to Caesar. Amongst them was Lucius Pupius, the senior centurion of his legion, who had formerly held that post in the army of Pompeius, and who was now brought by his men as a prisoner to Caesar. The latter, after congratulating Attius' troops upon their decision, dismissed Pupius, and, in thanking the townspeople of Osimo, told them he would not forget their conduct.

Meanwhile, in Rome, such a panic arose from the accounts of these operations, that the consul Lentulus, who had gone to open the treasury for the purpose of disbursing the money voted by the Senate to Pompeius, fled incontinently from the city, leaving the more sacred of the two treasuries[13] wide open, owing to a false alarm that Caesar was momentarily expected, and his cavalry already at the gates. He was at once followed by his colleague Marcellus, and by the majority of the other magistrates. Pompeius had left the capital the

day before, and was now on his way to the two legions taken from
Caesar, which he had distributed in winter quarters in Apulia. All
levying of troops was at once suspended in the vicinity of the city; no
place was thought safe north of Capua. Here, with their confidence
at last recovered, they rallied, and began to organize a levy among
the farmers lately settled as colonists in that district by the Julian
law;[14] and the consul Lentulus even went so far as to take the band
of gladiators maintained there by Caesar, and bring them out into
the market place, where, after inciting their hopes by the prospect
of earning their liberty, he gave them horses and placed them under
his orders. A subsequent hint, however, from his friends that this
proceeding was universally condemned, compelled him to distribute
them for custody amongst his acquaintances in the Capuan district.

Meanwhile Caesar, advancing from Osimo (*Auximum*), overran the
whole of the Marches of Piceno (*Picenum*). He was received with open
arms by all the country towns, who readily supplied his army with all it
needed. Even Cingolo (*Cingulum*), a town founded by Labienus,[15] and
built at his personal charges, sent a deputation to inform him what
great pleasure it would give them to receive his commands; and on his
ordering troops, sent them at once. By this time also the Twelfth legion
overtook him; and with these two he now advanced against Ascoli
Piceno (*Asculum Picenum*). That town was held by a force of ten battalions under Lentulus Spinther; but, on the news of Caesar's approach,
Spinther evacuated the place, and endeavored to take his battalions
with him. Deserted, however, by the larger number, he continued
his march with a mere handful, until he fell in with Vibullius Rufus,
who had lately come with a special commission from Pompeius to
strengthen the hands of his party in the Picenian lowlands. Vibullius,
on hearing from Spinther the state of operations in that quarter, took
over the latter's troops, and dismissed their commander. He then proceeded to concentrate as many units as he could from the Pompeian
levy in the surrounding districts, amongst which there joined him six
battalions under Lucilius Hirrus, whom he met flying from Camerino
(*Camerinum*) with what had formerly been the garrison of that city; and
in this way he succeeded in making up as many as thirteen battalions.
These he then led by forced marches to Domitius Ahenobarbus at
Pentima (*Corfinium*),[16] to whom he announced the near approach of

Caesar with two legions. Domitius himself, it should be added, had also collected a force of about twenty battalions from Albe (*Alba*), drawn from the country of the Marsi, Peligni, and neighboring districts.[17]

Continuing his advance, Caesar, after securing Fermo (*Firmum*), and giving orders, upon the expulsion of Lentulus, to search out the troops who had deserted that general, and to organize a levy, had halted one day at Ascoli (*Asculum*) to obtain supplies, and had then started for Pentima. Arrived here, he found five battalions, thrown forward by Domitius for that purpose, engaged in cutting the bridge that spans the river[18] at a distance of some three miles from the city. With this force Caesar's advanced patrols now came into contact, with the result that Domitius' men were driven from the bridge and retired upon the town. Caesar quickly had his legions across, and, halting near the city, pitched his camp close up to the walls.

On intelligence of his arrival, Domitius selected some of those conversant with the country, and induced them, by the offer of a large reward, to go with a letter to Pompeius in Apulia, conveying a strongly-worded appeal for succor. In it he declared his belief that with two armies, aided by the natural difficulties of the country, it would be an easy task to surround Caesar, and to sever his communications; failing this, the lives of himself and more than thirty battalions of men, as well as those of numerous senators and Roman knights would be endangered. In the interval he encouraged his own party, placed artillery on the walls, allotted each officer his special duties in the defense, and, in a public harangue to his troops, promised each man a farm of twenty-five acres out of his own landed property, with corresponding increase in the case of centurions and reservists.

About this time Caesar received information that the people of Salmone (*Sulmo*), a town seven miles from Pentima, were anxious to side openly with him, but were prevented by Quintus Lucretius, a senator, and Attius the Pelignian, who were holding it with a force of seven battalions. Accordingly Marcus Antonius was dispatched to the place with five battalions of the Thirteenth legion; with the result that the townspeople no sooner recognized the gleam of our standards than, throwing open their gates, they streamed out, soldiers and citizens alike, to welcome Antony. Lucretius and Attius meanwhile tried to escape by leaping from the walls; but Attius was caught and brought back to Antonius, whereupon he requested to be sent to Caesar. Thus, on the same day as he had come, Antony was able to return with the surrendered battalions, taking Attius along with him. The troops Caesar incorporated with his own army; Attius he dismissed without penalty.

Three days had now passed before Pentima, spent by Caesar in strongly fortifying a camp, in collecting provisions from the neighboring towns, and in awaiting the arrival of his remaining forces. Indeed, during these days he was joined, not only by the Eighth legion, but also by twenty-two battalions from the new levies in northern Italy, and some three hundred cavalry from the King of Noricum:[19] reinforcements which enabled him to form a second camp on another side of the town, which he put under the charge of Curio. On the following days he commenced the circumvallation of the city with fortified lines of entrenchment; and the work on this was all but finished just as the messengers sent to Pompeius got safely back.

As soon as Domitius had read the letter which they brought, he determined to suppress the truth, and openly announced in a council of war that Pompeius was about to make a rapid march to their relief, exhorting his staff not to despair, but to make every preparation for the defense of the town. To a few intimate friends he divulged the real answer, and began to lay plans for escape. When it was seen, however, that his looks did not accord with his words, and that his whole manner betrayed more haste and nervousness than had been usual with him on previous days; and further that, contrary to his ordinary habit, he now held long and secret conversations with his friends for discussing their mutual plans, while he shrank from attending the councils of war and from the society of his brother-officers, the truth could no longer be hidden or disguised. This was that Pompeius had written back, flatly declining to court certain disaster; and intimating that, as Domitius had locked himself up in Pentima in opposition to his own plans and wishes, he must now take any opportunity that offered for rejoining him with all his forces. It was, of course, to prevent this very step, that Caesar was drawing his blockading lines around the city.

When the scheme of Domitius became generally known amongst the troops in Pentima, they privately summoned an unauthorized

gathering among themselves at dusk; and using as their mouth-
piece one of their officers, together with the centurions and most
influential of their own rank, expressed their decision as follows. "They
found themselves blockaded by Caesar, whose siege-works and fortifications were all but finished. Their own general Domitius, trust and
confidence in whom had alone induced them to stay and hold the city,
had thrown them all over and was now meditating flight: under these
circumstances it was their duty to consult their own safety." From this
resolution the Marsi in the place at first strongly dissented, and seized
upon what was considered the most strongly fortified quarter of the
town. So bitter, indeed, grew the quarrel, that an attempt was made to
come to blows and to fight it out with weapons; but shortly afterwards
the envoys who were dispatched by each party to the other enabled the
Marsi to learn what they did not know before, viz. the contemplated
flight of Domitius. When this was once known, the two forces joined
hands, and fetching their general into the open, surrounded him with
a guard. They then sent representatives of their own body to Caesar,
with a message that they were prepared to open the gates, to obey his
orders, and to deliver Domitius alive into his hands.

On receipt of these overtures, Caesar at once felt the extreme
importance of taking possession of the town at the earliest possible
opportunity, and of transferring the battalions in it to his own camp.
There was always the chance of the garrison changing their minds,
either through bribery, or the recovery of their spirits, or by false
reports; grave events in war being often determined by the slightest of accidents. On the other hand, there was also the fear that the
entry of his troops at night might lead to excess and the looting of
the town. Under these circumstances, therefore, he gave the envoys a
cordial welcome, and then sent them back to their city; whilst to his
own men he issued orders closely to watch the gates and walls. He
further stationed troops on the incompleted siege works, not, as on
previous days, at fixed intervals, but in one continuous line of sentries
and pickets, so that the men could touch hands with each other and
thus cover the entire chain of works. Officers were sent round on
tours of inspection, strictly charged, not only to guard against sallies
by bodies of the enemy, but also to look out for any secret escape of

individuals. That night not a man slept in camp, however careless or indifferent he might otherwise be; but engrossed as all were in the now rapidly approaching crisis, they continued to debate in their own minds the various aspects of the issue, as they wondered what would happen to the Pentimians, to Domitius, to Lentulus, and the rest, and what fate was in store for each group.

About six o'clock in the morning Lentulus Spinther hailed our sentries and guards from the city wall, with the request that, if possible, he might be allowed an audience with Caesar. Leave being granted, he was sent out from the town under an armed escort of Domitius' troops, who took good care not to leave him until they had brought him safely into the presence of Caesar.

He began with an impassioned appeal for his own life, imploring Caesar to spare him, and reminding him of their longstanding friendship, and of Caesar's many kindnesses to himself—which indeed were considerable; including, as they did, his election to the pontifical college,[20] his appointment to the province of Spain at the end of his praetorship, and support in his canvass for the consulship. Caesar interrupted his speech by telling him he had not left his province as a brigand, but to defend himself against the insults of his opponents, and to restore to their legal position tribunes of the people who had been driven from their country for daring to uphold his rights: in a word, to reassert the freedom both of himself and of the Roman people, at present ground down by the despotism of a clique. Reassured by such language, Lentulus asked leave to return to the town, intimating that his own successful petition would be a comfort and encouragement to others as well, some of whom were so panic-stricken as to be obliged to contemplate laying violent hands on their own persons. His request was granted, and he then withdrew.

At daybreak Caesar gave orders for all senators and their sons, as well as all officers and Roman knights, to be brought before him. Of the senatorial order there appeared five representatives, viz. Lucius Domitius, Publius Lentulus Spinther, Lucius Caecilius Rufus, Sextus Quintilius Varus (Domitius' paymaster), and Lucius Rubrius: the others included a son of Domitius, together with many other young lads, and a considerable number of knights and borough councilors, who had been ordered out for the campaign from the local towns by Domitius. Arrived in his presence, Caesar first placed them out of reach of the abuse and gibes of his own men, and then addressed them in a few curt phrases, seeing that they had not had the grace, on their side, to acknowledge his own extraordinary leniency towards themselves: after that he released them all without condition. A sum of about £50,000, which Domitius had taken with him into Pentima and there deposited in the city chest, was presently brought out by the four city magistrates. It was at once returned to Domitius by Caesar, who was determined men should not say he had shown more self-restraint in dealing with their lives than with their property; although it was well known that this particular specie was in fact government money, received from Pompeius for the payment of the troops. Having settled these preliminaries, he gave orders for Domitius' men to take the oath of military allegiance to himself; and then on the same day, striking camp, completed a full day's march, after a stay at Pentima of altogether one week. An advance through the districts of Ortona, Lanciano, Termoli, and Larino (the *Marrucini, Frentani*, and *Larinates*) brought him into Apulia.

To return to Pompeius. On intelligence of the operations round Pentima, he had left Lucera (*Luceria*), and, marching through Canosa (*Canusium*), came down to Brindisi (*Brundisium*). The various contingents raised by the recent levy were ordered to concentrate upon this seaport from the different parts of the country; whilst, in addition, slaves and herdsmen were armed and mounted, till they made up a force of about three hundred horse. Lucius Manlius, one of the praetors, followed his leader in all haste with six battalions from Albe (*Alba*); whilst another praetor, Rutilius Lupus, brought three more from Terracina. Both these bodies came in sight of the distant cavalry of Caesar, commanded by Vibius Curius, and each, leaving the praetor to himself, went over to that officer. The same thing happened on the remaining stages of the march, some units falling in with Caesar's main column, others with his cavalry. In addition to this, the colonel commandant of engineers in the army of Pompeius, Numerius Magius of Cremona, was captured on the march, and conducted into the presence of Caesar. The latter at once sent him back to his own commander with the following message. "Hitherto he had been refused the opportunity of an interview; but he was now coming to Brindisi (*Brundisium*), and it was of the most vital public interest that he should have a conference with Pompeius; for it was impossible to make the same progress by exchanging proposals through the medium of others, as by a personal discussion on all the points at issue."

Soon after sending this message, he himself reached Brindisi at the head of six legions: three of these consisted of veterans, while the rest were composed of the recent levies, and had only been brought up to their full strength during the recent march. This represented all his force, since the surrendered army of Domitius had been sent straight away from Pentima (*Corfinium*) into Sicily. On arrival, he found that the two consuls had crossed to Durazzo (*Dyrrachium*) with the bulk of the Pompeian army, but that Pompeius himself was still at Brindisi with twenty battalions. It was impossible to discover whether the latter remained there for want of transports or whether his intention was to retain a hold on Brindisi, and to use this corner of Italy, with the opposite Greek coast, as a base for keeping command of the Adriatic; a course which would allow him to conduct hostilities simultaneously from either side. Fearing, however, that his opponent would not think it advisable to abandon Italy, Caesar determined to block the entrance to Brindisi harbor and render it impracticable for shipping. The method employed for this was as follows. Selecting the narrowest part of the harbor entrance, he built out from either shore, where the water was shallow, a sort of rough breakwater, carrying a broad level top. To this structure, as soon as the deeper water rendered further progress impossible, owing to the rubble no longer holding together, a couple of rafts were attached, each thirty feet square, one at either end, and made fast by four anchors from the four corners, so that no action of the waves could shift them. As soon as the first pair were completed and placed in position, others of similar dimensions were fastened in continuation, and over all a smooth surface of earth was laid, designed to give a free road to his men when charging to repel the enemy. Round the front and flanks of each raft were erected protection-hurdles and mantlets; whilst every fourth raft carried a two-storied tower to aid in beating off the assaults of the enemy's ships, or his attempts to set fire to the work.

Plan of Brindisi. (Brundisium.)

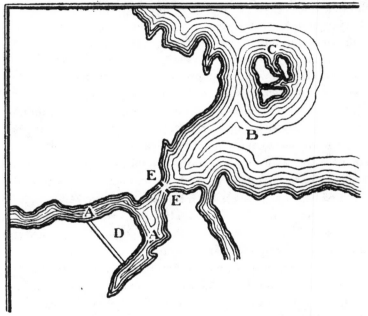

A A. Inner Harbour.　　　B. Outer Harbour.
C. Islands of St Andrea. (Ancient Barra.)
D. Town.　　　E E. Caesar's Moles.

To meet this device, Pompeius had recourse to a number of large merchantmen, which he had commandeered in Brindisi harbor. These vessels were specially fitted out by the erection on their decks of three-storied towers, armed with numerous pieces of artillery and every species of missile weapon. They were then driven against Caesar's works, with the object of breaking through the line of rafts and injuring the barricade; and daily engagements between the two parties, though not indeed at close quarters, were carried on by means of slings, arrows, and other similar weapons.

These operations, though necessarily demanding Caesar's most careful attention, did not, however, as yet cause him to despair altogether of peace. It was true that the failure of Magius to return, after being expressly sent with communications to Pompeius, caused him considerable misgiving; it was also true that his continued efforts in this direction gravely compromised his plans for taking military initiative: but notwithstanding all this, he felt himself bound to leave no stone unturned in the pursuit of his main object. He therefore dispatched one of his staff, Caninius Rebilus, a personal friend and relative of Scribonius Libo, with a commission to see that officer, and to beg to exert his influence for peace. Above all, he requested a personal conference with Pompeius, and again stated his firm conviction that if this could only be brought about, a peaceful solution, honorable to both parties, would be arrived at. Should this result be attained, most of the credit and reputation attaching to it would belong to Libo, whose active intervention would then have prevented a civil war. Libo went straight from this conversation with Caninius to Pompeius; only, however, to return with the message that, in the absence of the two consuls, no steps towards a settlement could be taken. With this last answer to efforts continually repeated, and repeated in vain, Caesar came to the reluctant conclusion that the time for such measures had now gone by, and that henceforward the war must be prosecuted with vigor.

The sea-mole he was building was about half finished, after nine days' work spent upon it, when the transports which had conveyed the van of the Pompeian army across to Durazzo (*Dyrrachium*) returned from the consuls, and safely entered Brindisi. Thereupon, whether it was that he became nervous at Caesar's blockading piers, or that his plan of campaign had all along been to let Italy go—at all events, with the arrival of these ships, Pompeius commenced preparations for evacuation. In order, however, to break the force of an attack from Caesar's troops, should the latter storm the town at the moment of withdrawal, he caused the city gates to be blocked up, barricaded the streets and thoroughfares of the town; whilst across the main arteries trenches were carried, bristling on the far side with sharp stakes and horizontally set piles, which were then carefully covered with light hurdles strewn with earth. All external approaches to the harbor, including two regular roads, were fenced off by driving into the ground enormous baulks carrying sharply pointed heads; and with these dispositions completed, orders were given for the legionaries to embark in silence; whilst on the walls and city towers was posted a thin line of light-armed troops, drawn from the reservists, archers, and slingers. These last were, at a prearranged signal, immediately the legionaries were all on board, to fall back upon a conveniently sheltered spot, where transports suitable for either sailing or rowing lay ready to receive them.

Now, the people of Brindisi, instigated by what they had suffered from the Pompeian soldiery, as well as by their contemptuous treatment at the hands of Pompeius himself, heartily espoused the cause of Caesar. As soon as the news, therefore, leaked out of this decision to sail, under cover of the confusion caused by the busy preparations of the troops, signals were made on all sides from houses in the town. Informed in this way of what was going forward, Caesar ordered his men to prepare scaling-ladders and to put on their arms, determined to lose no chance of striking an effective blow. At nightfall, however, Pompeius sailed. The guards left behind on the wall retired at the appointed signal, and rushed down to the ships by paths well known to themselves. Caesar's troops flung their ladders into position, and swarmed up the walls; but, warned by the townspeople against the sunken ditches and fenced dykes, they were forced to check their rush, and were then guided round to the harbor by a more circuitous route. Here, finding two of the transports with troops on board which had run upon the mole, they hauled them off by row-boats and launches, and then safely secured them as prisoners.

CHAPTER TWO

THE SAFEGUARDING OF THE WEST

WITH THE ESCAPE OF POMPEIUS AN ACCOMPLISHED FACT, THE PLAN that most commended itself to Caesar for settling the business between them was to collect transports, and cross over after his opponent before the latter could strengthen his position by raising large bodies of oversea auxiliaries. The delay, however, and length of time involved in this course was a serious consideration; for Pompeius, by requisitioning every ship on that part of the coast, had made immediate pursuit of himself impossible. The only alternative was to wait for vessels to come from the somewhat distant regions of Northern Italy and Piceno (*Picenum*), or from the Sicilian Straits; but this, owing to the unfavorable season of the year, appeared both a slow and precarious scheme. And, further, whilst he was waiting, the two Spanish provinces (one of which was devoted to the interests of Pompeius by reason of the great services he had rendered it), together with the veteran army stationed in them, would be steadily strengthened; auxiliary forces and cavalry would continue to be raised; and the allegiance of Gaul and Italy would be undermined, while he was out of the way; none of which proceedings he was at all disposed to allow.

For the present, therefore, he gave up the idea of pursuing Pompeius, and determined to transfer the war to Spain.[1] For this purpose orders were at once given to the governing magistrates of all municipal seaports to commandeer the required vessels, and have them brought round to Brindisi (*Brundisium*). With equal promptitude one of his staff, Valerius, was sent with a single legion to secure Sardinia; and Curio, with two legions and the powers of a governor, was similarly dispatched to Sicily, with orders to take his army over into Africa, immediately that island had been reduced. Sardinia was at the time held by Marcus Cotta, Sicily by Marcus Cato; whilst Tubero had been allotted Africa and was then due to take over the governorship. In Sardinia the people of Cagliari (*Carales*), as soon as they heard that Valerius was to be sent them, even before the expeditionary force had left Italy, of their own initiative expelled Cotta from the town; whereupon the Pompeian officer, frightened by the knowledge that the feeling of the province was unanimous, hastily quitted Sardinia for Africa. In Sicily Cato was busy repairing old men-of-war, and levying new ones from the various local communities; work into which he was throwing himself with extraordinary vigor. Special service officers had been sent to raise troops throughout Basilicata and Calabria (*Lucania* and *Bruttium*) from among those who held the Roman franchise; whilst in Sicily each township was required to furnish its fixed quota of horse and foot. These dispositions were all but completed when news reached the island of the approach of the rival governor Curio. Upon this report Cato summoned a general assembly, and in it openly denounced Pompeius for having deserted and betrayed his representative, and for having embarked on a war for which there had been no sort of necessity, without even the semblance of preparation; and that, in spite of the assurances publicly given in the Senate, in response to inquiries from himself and the rest, that everything was fully prepared for hostilities. With this last public protest he took a hurried farewell of his province.

Thus it was that when Valerius and Curio arrived with their armed forces in Sardinia and Sicily respectively, they each found a province bereft of its constituted authorities. Tubero, on the other hand, on reaching Africa, found that province in the hands of Attius Varus, who was there engaged in exercising full military command. This general, after losing his battalions at Osimo (*Auximum*) under the circumstances already described, had completed his flight by taking the first ship for Africa; and, the country being at the time without a governor, had appointed himself to the command. Here he organized a levy and succeeded in raising two entire legions; his knowledge of the locality and its inhabitants, and his familiarity with the province, opening a way for such considerable designs; he having a few years previously governed this province at the close of his praetorship. Thus, when Tubero arrived with his ships off Utica,[2] he found himself refused admission to either the harbor or town; not even his son, who was sick on board, was allowed to be landed, and he was obliged to weigh anchor and set sail from the neighborhood.

This was the point events had reached when Caesar, being desirous of resting his men from their recent hard work before commencing further active operations, made a distribution of his present forces among the neighboring Italian towns,[3] and then set out himself for the capital. Here having summoned the Senate, he made the House a statement of the wrongs he had suffered at the hands of his political adversaries. He reminded members that it was no unconstitutional position he had sought; he had waited the legal time for re-election to the consulship, and had shown himself content with what was within the reach of every citizen alike. A proposal, allowing him to stand in his absence, had been submitted to the people by all the ten tribunes, and there carried in the teeth of the violent opposition of his opponents, particularly that of Cato, who had characteristically employed his favorite trick of talking out time each day the assembly had met. This measure, he reminded them, had been adopted in Pompeius' own consulship;[5] why then, if the latter disapproved of it, did he allow it to be passed, or why, if he approved, had he prevented his (Caesar's) availing himself of the concession thus granted? He then asked the House to notice his own extraordinary forbearance in voluntarily proposing the disbandment of both armies, involving, as it would have done, a deliberate sacrifice of prestige and of his own legitimate position. He also exposed the bitter party-spirit betrayed by his antagonists, who did not hesitate to ask from another what they declined to do themselves; but sooner than yield up their command over standing armies preferred to plunge the whole world into war. The illegality of depriving him of the two legions was, moreover, openly denounced, along with the violent, high-handed action of curtailing the powers of the tribunate; nor did he omit to mention his own proposals for peace, and his repeated but thwarted attempts at an interview.

Under these circumstances he urged and invited them to take up, and to retain the reins of government in conjunction with himself. Did, however, they shrink from cooperation with him, through fear of the consequences to themselves, he would not inflict himself upon them, but would carry on the administration alone. Meanwhile, he considered representatives should at once be sent to Pompeius with a view to a settlement; for he felt no apprehension himself, like that lately uttered in the Senate by Pompeius, viz. that the opening of overtures by one party implied the recognition of the justice of the other party's claims, and a corresponding want of confidence in its own. That was but a weak and childish view of things. His own desire was to triumph by justice and equity, even as he had already sought to anticipate his opponent in action.

The idea of opening negotiations with Pompeius commended itself to the House; the difficulty was to find those willing to go. The chief reason for this general refusal to serve on such a commission was personal fear; since Pompeius, on evacuating the capital, had openly declared in the Senate that he would regard all who stayed behind in Rome in the same category as those actually within Caesar's camp. The result of this threat was that three whole days were now wasted in wrangling and excuses. Moreover, the party opposed to Caesar put up Lucius Metellus to frustrate this proposal, and at the same time to block all other business which Caesar had designed. Perceiving his object, therefore, and reflecting that he had already spent several wasted days, when he was determined not to lose more time, Caesar left his proposed measures unfinished, and, taking his departure from the city, traveled through to Further Gaul.[6]

Arrived here, he learnt that Pompeius had recently dispatched into Spain Vibullius Rufus, whom he had himself only a few days previously captured and released at Pentima (*Corfinium*): that Domitius had similarly gone off to seize Marseilles (*Massilia*) with seven fast ships of the mercantile marine that could either sail or row, which he had collected from private owners off the island of Giglio (*Igilium*) and in the harbor of Cosa, and there manned with his own slaves, freedmen, and small tenantry: and lastly, that some young nobles of

Marseilles, who had lately been in Rome, had been sent on home as envoys from Pompeius, with a strong appeal, given on the eve of his departure from the capital, that they would not allow the recent services rendered to their city by Caesar to obliterate the memory of his own past benefits. It was the receipt of this message that had induced the Massiliots to shut their gates against Caesar. They had further requisitioned the services of the Albici, a foreign tribe living in the hill country northeast of Marseilles, to which city they had long been subject: corn had been got in from the surrounding neighborhood and from all their fortified stations, for storage in the city; arsenals had been established for the manufacture of war material; and finally the walls and gates and fleet were now being put into repair.

Caesar requested the presence from Marseilles of the standing committee of fifteen chief councilors of the city; and on their arrival, pleaded with them not to allow their town to incur the responsibility of commencing hostilities, but to follow the unanimous decision of Italy rather than give ear to the wishes of a single individual. Other considerations which he thought calculated to bring them to their senses were also added; and the delegates departed to report his words, only, however, to return with the following resolution of their governing council. "The Roman world," they understood,

. . . was divided between two factions; but which of these had the better right was beyond their province and their power to decide. The leaders of these two parties (Pompeius and Caius Caesar) were both alike patrons of their city, which owed to one of them the annexation of the territories of the Arecomican Volcae and the Helvii,[7] and to the other an increase of their revenues by the incorporation of the Sallyae,[8] whose conquest he had effected. With such an equality in favors received, the proper return to make was a like impartiality in their own attitude; to give assistance to neither against the other, and to allow to neither access to their city or harbors.

These negotiations were still actively proceeding, when Domitius arrived with his squadron off Marseilles, to be at once admitted by the inhabitants, placed in command of the city, and given supreme

direction of the war. Acting upon his instructions, the fleet was sent
out to scour the seas in every quarter; and every merchantman they
could lay their hands upon was brought back into harbor, where any
that were found to be unsound in their rivets, timber, or rigging were
broken up and used for the equipment and repair of the others. All
the corn discoverable was commandeered for the public service, and
any other provisions or supplies were held in reserve against a possible siege of the town.

Such unwarrantable acts determined Caesar to order up three
legions to Marseilles. Upon their arrival, siege towers and shelters
were at once pushed forward against the walls with a view to the
assault of the town, and at the same time instructions were given for
a fleet of twelve warships to commence building at Arles (*Arelate*).
These last were put together and fitted out within a month of the
day the timber for them was felled; and upon their safe transference
to Marseilles, Decimus Brutus was appointed as their admiral by
Caesar, who thereupon took his departure from Marseilles, leaving
his general Caius Trebonius to superintend the operations on the
landward side.

During this period of preparation another general, Caius Fabius,
had been dispatched into Spain at the head of three legions, lately
distributed in winter quarters at Narbonne and its neighborhood,
with orders to seize without delay the passes of the Pyrenees, then
in the hands of Lucius Afranius, who held them for Pompeius. This
force was immediately to be followed by the remaining legions, then
wintering further away. In obedience to his orders, Fabius, acting
with great promptitude, dislodged the garrison from the pass before
him, and then marched rapidly upon the army of Afranius.

In Spain the arrival of Lucius Vibullius Rufus on a mission, as we
have seen, from Pompeius, had resulted in a conference of the three
Pompeian representatives, viz. Afranius, Petreius, and Varro; who
held respectively Eastern Spain with three legions, Western Spain, or
the territory between the Sierra di Morena and the Guadiana (*Castolo*
range and the *Anas*) with two more, and the country north of the
Guadiana (*Anas*), including Estremadura and Portugal (the *Vettones*
and *Lusitania*) likewise with two. At this conference they arranged
their own shares in the pending operations. Petreius was to march

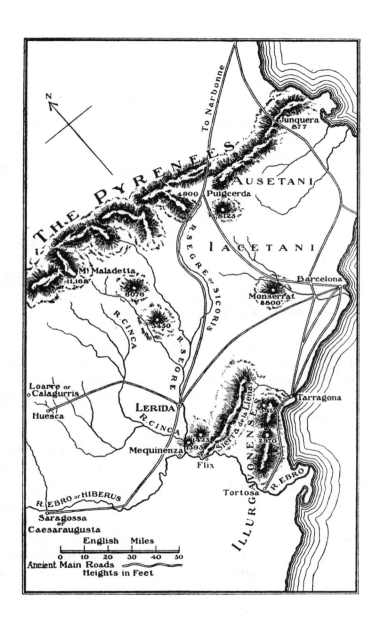

with his whole force from Portugal (*Lusitania*), through Estremadura (the *Vettones*), in order to join Afranius; whilst to Varro was allotted the defense of the whole of the western part of the Peninsula with the legions attached to his command. Having settled these preliminaries, they proceeded to raise cavalry and auxiliary troops; Petreius superintending the levy throughout Portugal (*Lusitania*), and Afranius that in Guadalajara and Avenca, Oviedo and Santander (*Celtiberia* and the *Cantabri*), and among all the barbarian tribes of the northwestern seaboard. Directly these were ready Petreius lost no time in passing through Estremadura to Afranius; and the two agreed to cooperate in the conduct of the war, and to make their head quarters at Lerida (*Ilerda*) on account of the great strategical importance of that place.

As stated above, Afranius had three legions and Petreius two; in addition to these there had now been raised in the Eastern province an infantry force armed with the oblong shield of regulars, and in the Western a similar force carrying the light round Spanish shield, the two bodies amounting in all to some eighty battalions; whilst each of the two provinces had also contributed some five thousand mounted men. As against these, Caesar's present field army consisted of six Roman legions. Of auxiliary infantry he possessed none; though he still retained with him the three thousand native cavalry which had served through all his late campaigns; and this force had lately been doubled by the addition of an equal number from Gaul, which he had himself personally raised by inviting individually to his standard the flower of the nobility and manhood in each of the Gallic communes. Finally, this body had been further strengthened by incorporating in it drafts from the splendid fighting races of Aquitaine, and from the hill tribes on the frontier of Provence. As for the probable course of the campaign, there had lately reached him a report to the effect that Pompeius, with his legions, was marching on Spain by way of Morocco (*Mauretania*), and was now rapidly approaching. It was at this time also that he borrowed money from his officers and centurions for distribution among the troops, a device by which two distinct objects were gained; on the one hand, the loyalty of his centurions was assured by the stakes he now held from them; on the other hand, such lavish liberality secured the interested devotion of the common soldiers.

Meanwhile Fabius was endeavoring to win the adhesion of the neighboring Spanish communes by addressing letters to their leaders, and by disseminating proclamations among the country folk. On the Segre (*Sicoris*) two bridges had been constructed, some four miles apart, over which foraging parties were now regularly proceeding, as everything on the westward side had been eaten up during the previous days. The same course of action was being pursued by the Pompeian generals, and for the same reason, thus giving rise to numerous cavalry skirmishes between the two forces. Two legions were accordingly sent over as a daily escort to the Fabian foragers; and on one occasion these had but just crossed by the lower bridge, and were being followed by the baggage and all the cavalry, when suddenly the heavy wind that was blowing, aided by the swollen state of the river, caused the bridge to snap, thereby leaving a section of the cavalry cut off on the farther side. Petreius and Afranius quickly realizing the situation from the hurdles and bridge-flooring that came swirling down the stream, the latter commander at once took over four legions and all his cavalry by the permanent bridge connecting the opposite bank with the town of Lerida (*Ilerda*) and his own camp, and then rapidly advanced against the two legions of Fabius. Their approach was reported to Lucius Plancus, the commanding officer for the day of the Fabian guard; and he immediately perceived the necessity of taking up a position on some high ground, where he drew up his men on a double front, in order to ensure himself from being surrounded by the enemy's horse. In this formation he received the attack, and, though vastly outnumbered, succeeded in beating off the fierce assaults of the legions and mounted troops. The engagement between the opposing cavalry had not long been in progress, when both sides caught sight in the distance of the advancing standards of two more legions. These proved to be reinforcements for ourselves, dispatched across the upper bridge by Fabius owing to his suspicion of what in fact had occurred, viz. that the enemy's generals would avail themselves of the opportunity thus offered them by fortune for crushing our intercepted detachment. Their arrival put an end to the action, and thereupon both sides withdrew into camp.

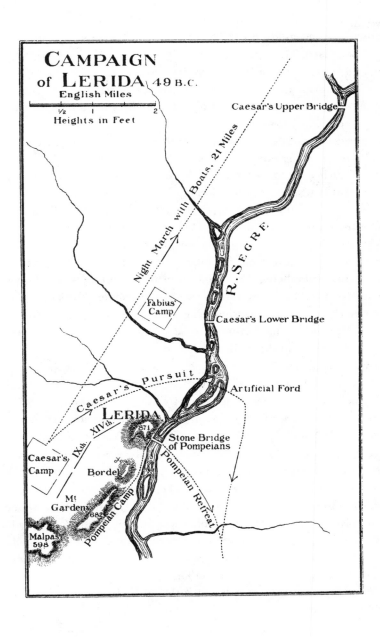

CAMPAIGN
of LERIDA 49 B.C.
English Miles
½   1   2
Heights in Feet

Caesar's Upper Bridge

Night March with Boats, 21 Miles

R. SEGRE.

Fabius' Camp

Caesar's Lower Bridge

Caesar's Pursuit

Artificial Ford

LERIDA
XIVth
IXth
571

Stone Bridge of Pompeians

Caesar's Camp

Bordel

Pompeian Retreat

Mt Gardeny
682
Pompeian Camp

Malpas
598

Two days after this event Caesar arrived at head quarters, accompanied by nine hundred cavalry which he had previously detained as a bodyguard. The bridge wrecked by the storm he found almost repaired, and at once gave orders for its completion during the night. He next informed himself of the nature of the surrounding country, and on the morrow, leaving a garrison of six battalions for the camp and bridge, together with all his baggage, drew up his entire force in three parallel columns, and marched straight upon Lerida, halting beneath the camp of Afranius. There he remained sometime in battle formation, in order to give Afranius an opportunity for coming down to engage him upon level ground. Afranius answered the challenge by moving out in force, but halfway down the hill halted under the protection of his fortified lines; whereupon Caesar, seeing it was Afranius who declined the combat, determined to entrench a camp about 400 yards from the lowest spurs of the fortress rock. To prevent his troops being thrown into confusion, whilst engaged upon its construction, by any sudden onset from the enemy which might force them to break off the work, he gave orders to omit the building of a rampart, which was bound to be seen at a distance by projecting above the level, and directed his men merely to dig a trench thirty feet wide along his front and parallel with the enemy. His first two lines then continued to stand to arms in their original formation, whilst behind them the work was secretly executed by the third; and by this device the whole business was finished off before Afranius discovered that a camp was being fortified under his very eyes. At the close of the day Caesar withdrew his legions inside this trench, and that night his men slept under arms.

On the morrow the whole army was kept within the same trench; and, since the earth necessary for a raised rampart would have to be fetched further afield, the same plan was, for the present, adopted in the work, a single legion being told off to the fortification of each of the three remaining sides of the camp, with orders to dig trenches of equal dimensions with the first. The three other legions were at the same time stationed in light embattled order fronting the enemy and ready for action. In this situation Afranius and Petreius, hoping to create a diversion and to hinder the construction of our earthworks, advanced their entire force down to the lowest spurs of the hill, thus menacing a general attack. They were not successful, however, in inducing Caesar to suspend the work, the latter having full confidence in the ability of the three legions to defend it, especially when aided by the protection of the trench; and so, after remaining in position for a short time, without ever advancing further than the base of the hill, they withdrew their troops back into camp.

The third day of his arrival before Lerida (*Ilerda*) saw Caesar's camp fortified with an earthen rampart; and on its completion, orders were at once given for the remaining battalions left behind at the earlier camp, together with all the baggage, to join the new head quarters.

Now between the town of Lerida and the hill which lies nearest it, on the heights of which Petreius and Afranius lay encamped, there stretched an open plain some 300 yards wide; and about halfway across this plain rose a gentle knoll,[9] the occupation and fortification of which would, Caesar was convinced, enable him to cut the enemy's communications with the town and bridge, and the immense quantity of stores they had there accumulated. In the hope of accomplishing this *coup*, he advanced three legions from camp; then, having drawn up his main line in a suitable position, he pointed to the hill and ordered the first ranks of one of the legions to dash forward and seize it. The movement was no sooner discovered by the enemy than the battalions of Afranius on picket duty before their own camp were sent by a shorter route to occupy the same ground. A fight ensued, and Afranius' men, coming up first to the hill, repulsed our detachment and compelled it, on the approach of further reinforcements, to turn and fall back upon the main body of the legions.

The type of fighting affected by the enemy's troops was to open with an impetuous charge, and boldly seize upon some good position. Little or no endeavor was made to preserve strict formation, fighting, as they did, in open and scattered order; whilst, if hard pressed, no scruples of military honor deterred them from falling back or evacuating their post. Residence with Lusitanians and other foreign tribes had familiarized them with this kind of warfare; for experience shows that troops generally conform in great measure to the customs of the country in which they have long been stationed. These tactics now occasioned much confusion amongst our men, who were quite unaccustomed to such a mode of attack. The isolated rushes of the enemy produced the belief that their unprotected flank[10] was being turned; whilst, on the other hand, it was a military tradition with themselves not to break their ranks, or to leave the standards, or surrender a position once occupied, except from the gravest causes. The result was that when the advanced ranks were driven in, the legion posted on that wing failed to stand its ground, and fell back upon the nearest hill.

The whole incident had been so unexpected and so exceptional, that practically the whole Caesarian line was swaying with unsteadiness. Rallying his men, Caesar led up the Ninth legion in support of his beaten detachment, which was now being hotly and triumphantly pursued by the enemy. His advance at once checked them, and compelled them in turn to take flight towards the town, where they halted just under the wall. But the men of the Ninth, carried away by the excitement of battle, in their eagerness to repair the loss sustained by their comrades, followed recklessly upon the protracted flight of the enemy, until they found themselves on ground that put them at considerable disadvantage, viz. at the foot of the hill on which stands the town of Lerida (*Ilerda*). On endeavoring to extricate themselves from this predicament, they were once more hard pressed by the enemy, who now held the advantage of position. The place was a precipitous one, with a perpendicular wall of rock on either side, and only of about sufficient width to accommodate three battalions in battle order; consequently no reinforcements could be sent up from either flank, nor could the cavalry afford them any relief in their distress. From the town the path descended with a gently falling slope some 600 paces long, and it was down this slope that our men had now to retire, through their inconsidered zeal in pressing the pursuit so far; and here a most unequal fight had to be maintained. For not only was the path inconveniently narrow, but the enemy had halted immediately under the shoulders of the rock, and could therefore make every discharge tell with effect upon our troops. In spite of this, the latter fought on with unflinching courage, patiently enduring the many wounds inflicted upon them. The Pompeians were presently rein-forced, and additional battalions were constantly dispatched from their camp and pushed up through the town, thereby allowing fresh troops to replace those who were exhausted. This movement Caesar was also obliged to adopt, and to send up fresh battalions into the same cul-de-sac, in order to withdraw his wearied men.

After five uninterrupted hours of this kind of combat, the Caesar-ian troops, finding themselves sorely pressed by superior numbers, and having now exhausted their supply of spears, drew swords and charged uphill into the serried masses of the enemy, where, hurling some over the rocks, they compelled the others to turn and run. Forcing them up against the city wall, they even drove a section through panic into the town, until by this vigorous action they had procured for themselves an unmolested retreat. During this interval the cavalry also, after being obliged to halt on the rocky ground lower down, had managed on both flanks by splendid efforts to work its way up the hillside, where by riding up and down between the two hostile lines, it ensured a more undisturbed and safer retirement for the legionaries.

The battle was thus one of varying fortunes. Our losses at the first collision were about seventy killed, including Quintus Fulginius, a centurion of the third company[11] in the first battalion of the Four-teenth legion, who had reached that position from the lower grades through conspicuous gallantry in the field; whilst the wounded num-bered over six hundred. On the side of the Afranians Titus Caecilius, the first centurion of his legion, together with four other centurions, were killed, as well as over two hundred rank and file.

The general opinion entertained about the day's events showed that each party claimed to have left the field as victors. The Afranians appealed to the fact that, though considered by common consent to be inferior troops to those of the enemy, they had nevertheless stood up to their attack for a considerable length of time; not to mention that in the early part of the day they had secured their position at the knoll which had been the original cause of the engagement, and at this first encounter had actually compelled their enemy to turn and fly. On the other hand, our men could show that, with both ground and numbers against them, they had notwithstanding maintained a steady resistance of five long hours, at the end of which they had stormed the hill, and at the point of the sword dislodged the enemy from his vantage-ground, putting him to flight and even driving him into the town.

As a consequence of this engagement, the hill, for the possession of which the battle had been waged, was now strongly fortified by the Pompeians, and a garrison established on it.

Two days after these events there suddenly occurred a further misfortune. A storm of exceptional severity arose; indeed, the floods that ensued were admittedly unprecedented for those regions. On this occasion the rain also washed down the snow from all the hills, causing the river to overflow, and smashing on one and the same day both the bridges erected by Caius Fabius. This last circumstance caused the gravest inconvenience to Caesar's army; for his camp being built, as already explained, between the two rivers Segre and Cinca (*Sicoris* and *Cinga*), a space only thirty miles wide, now that neither of these two was passable, the whole of his forces were inevitably penned in between their narrow barriers. Outside too, not only were the native states which had joined him unable to bring up provisions for the army, but bodies of his own troops, who had been away on distant foraging parties, saw themselves cut off by the swollen rivers and powerless to return; whilst immense convoys now coming from Italy and Gaul found it impossible to get through to camp. Further to aggravate matters, it was an especially awkward period of the year: the supplies in the magazines of the winter camps had now run out, and the new year's corn was not quite ripe. In addition to this, the native Spanish communes had already been drained dry; for Afranius had, before Caesar's arrival, collected into Lerida nearly all the corn in their hands, any that remained having been subsequently consumed by Caesar himself; whilst the cattle belonging to the neighboring communities, which at such a time of scarcity might have proved a useful substitute, had all been removed to a distance by their owners on account of the war. The result was that the parties who were away foraging for corn and provender were now harassed by light-armed Lusitanians, and by the light Spanish infantry from the Eastern province. These men not only knew every inch of the ground, but found no difficulty in swimming any river, since they never go on active service without taking their air-bladders along with them. On the other hand the Afranian army had abundant supplies of every kind. Steps had early been taken to amass large stocks of corn, and this was still being largely increased from every quarter of the province: similarly of forage there were unlimited supplies. Lastly the bridge at Lerida afforded ample facilities for collecting all such stores, and gave them a wholly untapped source of supply in the country east of the Segre (*Sicoris*), from which of course Caesar was completely excluded.

These floods lasted several days. Caesar made attempts to repair the bridges, but the volume of water would not allow of it, and, moreover, the pickets of the enemy that lined the opposite bank rendered their completion impossible. It was indeed an easy task for these latter to prevent the work of construction, since, besides the state of the river itself and the quantity of water we had to deal with, they were in a position to concentrate all their spears upon a single narrow point from the whole line of bank; and it was a difficult matter for our people to carry on the engineering works in the midst of a boiling stream, and at the same time to avoid the weapons hurled at them.

Meanwhile Afranius received intelligence that the large convoys on their way to Caesar had halted at the river. Those who had thus arrived were in the first place a body of archers from the tribe of the Ruteni (*Rodez*), with a force of cavalry from the old province of Gaul, accompanied by numbers of wagons and a huge baggage-train, in the true Gallic fashion; besides these a heterogeneous collection of some six thousand persons, including the sons and servants of their masters. These unwieldy numbers exhibited no sort of internal arrangement, and possessed no recognized authority; but everybody followed his own private caprice, and the whole party was traveling without the slightest misgiving, and in full enjoyment of the freedom which previous journeys in the past had made habitual with them. Many of them were young men of distinguished families, sons of senators, and already members of the equestrian order; there were also delegates from various communities, and even some officers of Caesar; all of whom now found themselves alike hemmed in by the rivers.

To smash them, therefore, while in this predicament, Afranius undertook a night march with all his mounted forces and three of his legions; his cavalry being sent on ahead to deliver a surprise attack. But though surprised, the Gallic horse were quickly in their places, vigorously giving battle to the enemy. As long as the affair could be one between similar arms, their small force was quite a match for the large numbers of the Afranians; but the approaching standards of the legions caused them to beat a retreat to the nearest hills, after losing a few of their number. It was this part of the engagement that proved an invaluable diversion for securing the safety of the rest of the party, who used the respite thus gained to make for the higher ground. The day's losses amounted to some two hundred of the archers and a few of the horse, together with a slight number of camp followers and some of the baggage.

All these causes, however, resulted in a serious rise in the price of corn, which is generally inflated, not merely by present scarcity, but also by apprehensions for the future. It had now touched 150 shillings a bushel, and the want of farinaceous food had already lowered the physique of the troops, whose distress was increasing daily. Indeed, the last few days had produced such a complete revolution in the general position, and such a striking change of fortune, that, whilst our own men were suffering from the want of common necessaries, the enemy, with their unlimited supplies of every kind, were already being regarded as the winning side. Caesar accordingly turned for help to those townships which had already declared in his favor, and as their stocks of corn were so low, requisitioned cattle instead; the sutlers of the army were got rid of by being sent away to the more distant communities; and at the same time he personally took steps to alleviate the present distress by every device in his power.

Exaggerated and glowing accounts of the present military situation were now sent home to their supporters in Rome by Afranius, Petreius, and their party; and being further magnified by popular rumor, produced the impression that the war was virtually over.

On the arrival of these letters and messages in Rome, large crowds flocked to the house of Afranius with the most profusive congratulations. Numbers prepared to cross over from Italy to Pompeius; some from a desire to be regarded as the harbingers of such good news, others to avoid the appearance of having first waited to learn the issue of the war, or again of seeming to be quite the last to come in.

In this critical position, with all the roads blocked by Afranius' cavalry and infantry, and the bridges impossible to repair, Caesar directed his troops to build a number of boats, of a type which had become familiar to him in recent years from the method followed in Britain. The keels and main framework of these consisted of light timber, whilst the hull was constructed of plaited osiers lined outside with hides. When finished, these coracles were laid upon linked wagons, and carried upstream by a night march twenty-one miles from camp. Troops were then conveyed in them across the river, and at once proceeded to seize a hill which sloped down to the edge of the bank; and before the enemy had wind of the affair this hill was rapidly fortified. A whole legion was subsequently ferried over to the same point, and a fresh bridge commenced from either bank and finished off in two days. By this means Caesar succeeded in recovering his convoys and foraging parties in safety, and thereby at once relieved the strain upon his commissariat.

The same day that the bridge was completed, a large force of cavalry was thrown across the stream. Delivering a surprise attack upon the enemy's foragers, who were scattered about the country without the slightest apprehension, they headed off a considerable number of animals and men; and, on the approach of several battalions of Spanish light infantry sent to their relief, skilfully divided their forces, one division taking charge of the spoil, whilst the other remained to meet and repulse the advancing enemy. One of these battalions rashly broke its line, and charged ahead of the others; whereupon it became severed from its supports, was surrounded, and cut to pieces. The whole body of cavalry then returned to camp by the same bridge, bringing with them a large quantity of booty, and without having lost a single man.

CHAPTER THREE

THE FIRST NAVAL ENGAGEMENT

DURING THESE OPERATIONS AT LERIDA THE INHABITANTS OF Marseilles (*Massilia*), acting upon the advice of Lucius Domitius, fitted out a squadron of seventeen warships, eleven of which were decked boats. These were further increased by the addition of several smaller craft, in the hope of frightening our fleet by mere numbers. On board these ships was placed a strong force of archers, together with large drafts of the already mentioned Albici, whose courage was then incited by means of bribes and promises. A certain number of vessels Domitius claimed to be allowed as his own; and these he manned with the tenant farmers and herdsmen whom he had brought with him from Italy. The fleet, being thus fully equipped, sailed out with all confidence to meet our squadron, which under the command of Decimus Brutus was then lying at its base off an island that faces Marseilles.[1]

Brutus was far the weaker in number of ships; but, on the other hand, Caesar had appointed to this fleet, as its fighting crews, the *élite* of all his army, especially picked for their personal courage from each of his several legions, comprising front-rank soldiers and centurions, who had all begged to be allowed to undertake this particular duty. These crews had now prepared grappling-irons and boat-hooks, and provided themselves with an unlimited supply of heavy legionary and similar javelins, as well as the other lighter kinds of spears. As soon, therefore, as they had intelligence of the enemy's advance, they rowed their ships out of harbor, and gave battle to the Massiliots. The fight was conducted with the fiercest valor on either side. The Albici yielded little or nothing in bravery to our own men, being a race of hardy mountaineers, habituated to war; moreover they had only just parted from the Marseilles people, and still carried the promises these had made them fresh in their memory. Similarly, the herdsmen of Domitius mentioned above, with the hope of liberty as their incentive, were burning to prove their mettle beneath the eyes of their master.

The Massiliots themselves, relying on the speed of their ships and the skill of their steersmen, continued for sometime to elude our attempts at attack by suddenly shifting their helm whenever our vessels bore down upon them. As long as they had sufficient sea room, they remained strung out in a single long line, directing all their efforts to surrounding us, or trying to concentrate two or more ships against one of our own; or again, wherever they had a chance, they would endeavor to dash past our sides and to rip off the blades from our banks of oars. But when closer quarters became inevitable, and the skillful maneuvers of their helmsmen no longer availed them, it was to the fighting power of their mountaineers that their hopes were next directed. On the other hand, our people had to make shift with ill-trained oarsmen and less expert captains at the helm, men who had been suddenly transferred out of merchantmen, and who hardly knew even the names of the fittings of a man-of-war. They were also handicapped by the slow pace and great weight of their ships, which, having been hurriedly built from green wood, had not yet attained the same adaptability for rapid movement as those confronting them. Under these conditions as long as they were allowed a hand-to-hand fight, they had no hesitation in running their single ships in between two of the enemy; when, by letting go the grappling-irons, they would make both these fast to their own, one on either beam, and each crew then fighting in two divisions would board the two vessels alongside. By these tactics they inflicted heavy losses upon the Albici and herdsmen, and succeeded in sinking a part of the squadron, capturing others with their crews, and driving back the remainder into port.

As a result of the day's engagement the Massilians lost altogether nine of their vessels, this number including those which were captured.

CHAPTER FOUR

THE REWARD
OF A GREAT STRATEGIST

NEWS OF THIS BATTLE DULY REACHED CAESAR AT LERIDA, AND, taken in conjunction with the completion of the bridge, caused a speedy reaction in the fortunes of the campaign. For the Pompeians, through wholesome dread of the quality of our cavalry, now showed far less freedom and confidence in moving about the country. Some days they would come out only a short distance from camp, so as to have a quick means of retreat (a plan which confined their foraging to somewhat narrow limits); at other times they would make a long detour, and so avoid the pickets waiting for them; sometimes a slight brush with the enemy, or even the sudden appearance of our cavalry on the skyline, would make them drop their loads upon the spot and scurry back to camp. Latterly they had taken to doing their foraging at intervals of several days, and even by night; this last surely an unprecedented course for a commander to adopt.

Meanwhile the people of Huesca and Loarre (*Calagurris*), (the latter being politically incorporated with the former town), sent representatives to Caesar to put themselves at his disposal. They were followed at once by those of Tarragona (*Tarraco*), the Iacetanians and Ausetanians on the Mediterranean litoral, and a few days later by the Illurgavonensians from the southern bank of the Ebro. From all alike he requested help in the shape of corn. This they at once provided, and hunting up every pack-animal in the district, sent it forthwith into camp. The battalion of the Illurgavonensians serving with the enemy, on hearing of this decision of its tribe, actually deserted to Caesar, bringing over its standards from the post where they were quartered. Far-reaching indeed, and most rapid, was the revolution now effected. With the bridge completed, with five powerful tribes secured as friendly, with the commissariat once more working smoothly, and the rumors as to the alleged advance of Pompeius through Morocco (*Mauretania*) with a relieving force of legionaries finally disposed of, many of the more distant cantons now began to break their connection with Afranius, and to declare on the side of Caesar.

All these circumstances produced the greatest consternation in the ranks of his opponents, and Caesar determined to profit by it. With the object of putting an end to the necessity of always sending his cavalry by a long detour across his new bridge, he selected a suitable spot up-stream, and proceeded to dig a number of canals thirty feet wide, which, by drawing off part of the waters of the Segre (*Sicoris*) would create a ford over that river. These were on the point of completion, when Afranius and Petreius became seized with the utmost concern lest they should find themselves absolutely cut off from either corn or forage, on account of the overwhelming force of Caesar's cavalry. They therefore decided to anticipate this contingency by evacuating that part of the country, and transferring the seat of war to central Spain (*Celtiberia*). What further contributed to the adoption of this plan was the fact that, of the different Spanish states which had taken opposite sides in the late war with Sertorius,[1] the vanquished party had nothing but dread for the name and rule of Pompeius, even though an absentee governor: those, on the other hand, who had remained loyal now felt the warmest affection towards the man who had so greatly advanced their own interests; whilst as to Caesar, his name did not carry the same familiarity in the ears of foreigners as did that of his rival. Moreover, in these quarters they were expecting further large bodies of cavalry and native auxiliary infantry; and, once on their own ground, their idea was to prolong the campaign until winter had set in. In execution of this scheme, orders were given to collect boats all along the Ebro (*Hiberus*), and to bring them to Octogesa, a town on that river, twenty miles south of their present camp. A bridge of boats was then ordered to be built at that place, whilst two legions were moved across the Segre and a camp fortified on its farther bank as a *tête-de-pont* with an earth rampart twelve feet high.

Intelligence of these movements duly reached Caesar by means of his spies. The work of draining the river was accordingly pushed on without intermission day and night alike, the men straining every nerve. It had now advanced far enough for the cavalry to cross; and these did not hesitate to swim their horses over, although it was an operation fraught with the utmost difficulty, and indeed was but barely possible. But the infantry were still up to their shoulders, nearly neck deep, and were hindered from crossing, not merely by the depth of the water, but also by the rapidity of the current. Yet notwithstanding these difficulties, there was no appreciable interval between the news of the approaching completion of the bridge over the Ebro and the discovery of a ford at the Segre.

This last event made the enemy consider it advisable to hasten their departure. Leaving a guard of two auxiliary battalions at Lerida, they crossed the Segre in full force, and proceeded to camp in conjunction with the two legions that had crossed a few days earlier. The only course now left to Caesar was to employ his horse to harry and distress the retreat of his opponents. To use his own bridge for transporting his infantry involved a long detour, which would inevitably allow the enemy to reach the Ebro by a very much shorter route. The cavalry were therefore dispatched across the river, and, after crossing by the ford, suddenly appeared in the dark on the rearguard of the Pompeians (they had marched shortly after midnight), and, deploying in great force, endeavored to check and disorganize the retreat.

At dawn it could be seen, from some high ground near Caesar's camp, that our men were delivering a furious attack on the skirts of the enemy, and that the whole of their rearguard was occasionally held up and separated from the main body; whilst every now and then the Pompeians would take the offensive, and our people would be repulsed by a combined charge of all their regiments; only, however, to resume the assault as soon as our opponents turned their backs. Inside the camp the troops collected into knots, indignant at seeing the enemy thus slip from their grasp and the war unnecessarily prolonged. Approaching the centurions and officers, they implored these to tell Caesar not to think of sparing them either trouble or danger, but to assure him that they were quite ready and able, and fully prepared to venture on the passage of the stream where the cavalry had already crossed. Moved by their ardent representations, Caesar decided that the attempt should be made, in spite of the apprehensions he felt at exposing his army to such a body of water. Orders were given to weed out from every company any whose courage or strength seemed likely to prove unequal to the ordeal. These were left behind with a single legion to hold the camp, and the remaining force then marched out of their old quarters in light battle equipment. Arrived at the river, numbers of transport animals were strung across the stream, both above and below the ford, and when every precaution had thus been taken the passage of the army was successfully accomplished. Of the troops who took part in this enterprise a few were carried down by the force of the stream; but all were caught and rescued by the improvised cavalry, whilst of casualties there was not one.

With the army safely landed, the whole force fell into position and commenced to advance in three lines; and so great was the enthusiasm of the troops, that, although they had an additional six miles to do between camp and the ford, and were further greatly delayed at the river, they yet succeeded in overtaking before three o'clock in the afternoon those who had marched about one on the previous morning.

As soon as their approach was descried on the horizon by Afranius and Petreius, the former general, astounded at the amazing sight, at once halted on some rising ground and drew up for battle. Caesar, however, not wishing to send his men exhausted into action, halted in the plains to rest his army; but on the enemy once more attempting to advance, he renewed his harassing pursuit. They had therefore no option but to pitch camp sooner than otherwise had been their design. For the truth was they were now approaching a range of hills, and five miles further on they would come to difficult and

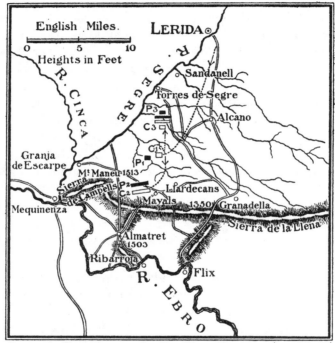

Caesar's Pursuit...........C1, P1, First Position (c.c. 65-67)
C2, P2, Position after Caesar's turning movement (c.c. 70, 71)
C3, P3, Position after the Retreat on Lerida (c.c. 81-83)

narrow roads. These hills it was their great object to penetrate, since their possession would not only deliver them from Caesar's cavalry, but also enable them, by holding the passes in his face, to bar the further progress of his army, and meanwhile to effect the passage of the Ebro (*Hiberus*) without danger or fear of molestation to themselves. The plan was one which they were bound to attempt and to carry out at all hazards: nevertheless, the fatigue consequent upon a whole day's battle and the heavy exertions of the march induced them to postpone it until the morrow. Caesar also then camped on the nearest high ground.

About midnight information reached him through some prisoners who had strayed too far from camp after water and had been caught by our cavalry, that the Pompeian generals were silently withdrawing from their intrenchments; whereupon the bugle was at once ordered to be sounded, and the command for striking camp to be proclaimed in the usual military fashion. The enemy, hearing the sound, and dreading lest they should be forced to fight at night when under the weight of their heavy marching kit, or again that they might be hemmed in amongst the narrow defiles by Caesar's horse, at once arrested their movement, and kept their forces in camp. The next morning Petreius made a secret expedition with a small party of mounted men to examine the lie of the land, and a similar party left Caesar's camp, under the command of Lucius Decidius Saxa, also to reconnoitre the country. Both parties reported in the same terms, viz. that for the first five miles the road ran through a plain, which was then succeeded by rugged mountain tracts; and that the side which got first to the passes could easily check the other's further advance.

A council of war having been summoned, a discussion was opened by Petreius and Afranius and the question raised as to the best time for making a start. The general opinion favored a night march, holding it quite possible to reach the passes without being detected. Others pointed to the orders for marching, which they had heard the previous night in Caesar's camp, as a proof that a surreptitious departure was out of the question. Evidently Caesar's cavalry surrounded them at night, holding all the roads and neighborhood, and night engagements were to be avoided, because in civil war, when a panic took place, troops generally obeyed the instincts of fear rather than those of discipline. Daylight, on the contrary, possessed a power in itself of bringing before the eyes of all men a keen fear of disgrace, which was greatly aided too by the presence of their officers and centurions; and it was these incentives that usually restrained troops and kept them to their duty. Hence on all grounds the attempt to break through should be made by day; for even though they might encounter some slight casualties, yet the desired position could quite well be captured without endangering the safety of the main army.

This last view prevailed in the council, and it was determined to make a start at daybreak on the following morning.

Meanwhile Caesar had carefully explored the locality, and with the first streak of dawn led his whole force out of camp. Their march took them by a long detour over roads that were little better than tracks, as all the main routes leading to the Ebro (*Hiberus*) and Octogesa were necessarily blocked by the enemy, whose camp lay across their path. Caesar's army had therefore to traverse a series of deep and difficult valleys, where the road was often rendered impracticable by precipitous rocks; so much so that the men's arms and accoutrements had to be passed along from hand to hand, and much of the march was only accomplished by the troops shouldering one another up after thus freeing themselves of their armor. Yet no one was heard to complain of the severity of the toil, well knowing, as they did, that all their toils alike would end, could they once succeed in barring the enemy from the Ebro, and in cutting his supplies.

The Afranian troops, in their joy, at first ran out from camp to see the sight, flinging after their retreating enemy many a parting taunt to those who now found themselves without enough to eat, and therefore obliged to go back to Lerida. And, indeed, there was some justification for their gibes; for the route led clean away from our objective, and thus made us seem to be marching in exactly the opposite direction. Their generals also began congratulating themselves on their own decision to remain in camp, and not too without much apparent reason: they could see that our pursuit had been undertaken without camp-animals or baggage, and naturally felt convinced that we could no longer hold out against the scarcity of food. When, however, they perceived that our column was gradually bending round to the eastward, and observed that its head was already abreast of the position occupied by their own camp, the most lethargic and indolent amongst them were found demanding instant departure and a race to overtake us. The call sounded to arms; and, leaving behind a few garrison battalions, the entire force turned out of camp and headed straight for the Ebro.

It was a contest in speed, and speed only, viz. which of the two parties could first seize the pass and mountain range. Caesar's army was retarded by the difficulties of the roads; Afranius' force was continually checked by the pursuing Caesarian cavalry. On the other hand, this last action of the Afranians had brought the situation to this inevitable conclusion—that should they be the first to reach the mountains ahead of them, although they might escape their own peril, they must none the less lose the baggage of their entire army, as well as their battalions left in camp; for these were now absolutely cut off by the intervention of Caesar's army from even the slightest possibility of relief. Caesar covered the distance first, and finding a sort of plateau as he emerged from the lofty rocks, drew up his line of battle on it in face of the enemy. Afranius, seeing his rearguard hard pressed by the Caesarian horse, and the enemy on his front, selected some high ground and there halted. From thence he dispatched a force of four Spanish light infantry battalions towards what was the dominating hill in all the surrounding country, with orders to advance at full speed and occupy it; his design being to follow in force himself, and, changing his first plan, to make for Octogesa by another route over the hills. The light infantry were hastening by a flank approach towards their objective, when they were discovered by Caesar's cavalry and at once attacked. The Spaniards were never for a moment equal to withstanding the fierce onset of our horse, but were quickly surrounded, and all cut to pieces in sight of both armies.

It was an opportunity such as rarely falls to the lot of a commander. Caesar was well aware that, after so terrible a disaster enacted before their very eyes, the enemy's army would be too shaken to offer much resistance, especially as they were completely dominated by his cavalry, who would be able to act with effect on the level and open ground where the conflict must be decided. To seize this opportunity was now the universal petition addressed to him. Generals, centurions, regimental officers—all alike came running up with the request that he would not hesitate to give battle. They pointed out that the men's ardor was strung to the highest pitch, whilst the Afranians, on the other hand, had given many proofs of a state of panic: first of all in failing to go to the relief of their own troops, then in declining to leave their hill; as well as in the fact that they could scarcely succeed even in keeping off the attacks of the cavalry, but were crowding together, with their standards mingled in confusion, not keeping to their own colors, or observing their proper ranks. They added, that if the enemy's advantage in position made him hesitate, an opportunity for a fight somewhere or other would doubtless soon arise, since Afranius would have to come down from the place, as he could not stay there without water.

On his side, Caesar had conceived a hope of being able to attain his purpose without a battle, and without bloodshed to his own troops, now that he had succeeded in cutting his opponents' supplies. Why, he asked himself, should he lose any of his men, even in a successful engagement, and why expose to the chance of wounds troops who had served him so magnificently? What right again had he to tempt Fortune, especially considering that a commander's duty is to effect his conquests by strategy no less than by the sword? Compassion also swayed him for his fellow countrymen, whose slaughter he could not but foresee; and he preferred to gain his ends with these men safe and sound. However, this plan did not commend itself to the majority; the troops were even heard declaring amongst themselves that, if such a golden opportunity for victory was to be thrown away, they would not fight even when Caesar wanted them. Nevertheless, he stood to his decision, and accordingly drew off a little from his present ground with the object of relieving the tension on his frightened opponents; whereupon Petreius and Afranius, profiting by the occasion, retreated to their old camp. Caesar then proceeded to post pickets and guards along the hills; after which, with every road to the Ebro (*Hiberus*) securely barred, he fortified a camp as close up to that of his enemy as was practicable.

On the morrow the commanders of the Pompeians, distracted at seeing all hope now gone of securing supplies or of reaching the Ebro, held a consultation on their future plans. There were only two roads open to them—one to Lerida, if they chose to return there, another if they made for Tarragona (*Tarraco*). In the midst of the discussion, a report was brought in that our cavalry were attacking their watering party. The report being confirmed, a guard was immediately posted in the shape of a series of pickets drawn from the cavalry and native infantry, and supported by battalions of the legions; and this step was then followed by orders to run up a rampart between camp and the watering place, so that the watering might proceed behind the earthwork without fear of molestation or need of any further guard. The supervision of this breastwork Petreius and Afranius decided to share between themselves, and in order to see it executed went out some considerable distance from their fortified lines.

Their departure afforded their men an uninterrupted opportunity for a talk with those in the opposite camp, and, flocking out, they proceeded to hunt up and hail any acquaintance or fellow townsman each happened there to possess. The first thing was a general expression of thanks to all our men for having spared them the day before when in their state of panic: their lives, they declared, they owed to this act of clemency. Next, they wanted to know what trust could be reposed in the others' commander; whether they would do right to put themselves in his power; following up this by a regret that they had not done so at first, instead of taking arms against their friends and blood relations. Encouraged by these conversations with our men, they next put forward a petition to the Caesarian general to spare the lives of Petreius and Afranius, being anxious to avoid the appearance of having committed the crime of betraying their own officers. Reassured on this point, they then declared they would come over at once, and proceeded to authorize their leading centurions to go as peace delegates to Caesar. While these were thus engaged, many of the Pompeians invited their Caesarian friends and took them back to their own camp, whilst others of themselves were taken off to ours; in a word, the unification of the two camps appeared complete. Numbers of regimental officers also and centurions came and tendered their allegiance to Caesar. The same course was taken by the Spanish chieftains whom the enemy had summoned to the campaign, and now held as hostages in their own camp. These men applied to their acquaintances and any with whom their families visited, to ensure for them each a favorable introduction to Caesar. The young son of Afranius was likewise engaged in negotiating with Caesar, through the help of the general Sulpicius, for his own and his father's life. On all sides were heard rejoicing and congratulation; since it looked as if the one party had escaped a dire peril, and the other gained a wonderful achievement without so much as a scratch. Everybody admitted the greatness of the reward which Caesar's undeviating clemency had brought him, and his recent decision was now universally applauded.

The report of these novel proceedings brought Afranius back from the earthwork then in course of construction, and he arrived in camp fully prepared, as was believed, to acquiesce without demur in whatever turn events might have taken. Petreius, on the contrary, never lost his presence of mind. Arming his retinue of private servants, and also taking with him the light Spanish infantry battalion that acted as the commander-in-chief's bodyguard, together with a small squadron of specially privileged native cavalry which were always about his person, he suddenly galloped up to the rampart, stopped the intercourse between the two armies, and drove our men out of his camp, putting any whom he caught to the sword. The rest drew together, and, appalled by the sudden peril, wrapped their left hands in their cloaks, and drawing their swords protected themselves as best they could against the horsemen and Spaniards. The nearness of their own camp lent them confidence; and, as they approached it, the pickets on guard outside advanced to their relief.

Having effected so much of his purpose, Petreius next made the round of the companies, appealing to the troops with tears in his eyes, and beseeching them not to betray him to the tender mercies of his foes, and not to betray their own absent commander Pompeius.

A general move was at once made towards head quarters. There he demanded that every man in camp should solemnly swear not to desert or betray the army or its chiefs, and not to enter upon any secret course of action on his own authority. This oath he first of all took himself, and then administered to Afranius. They were followed by the regimental officers and centurions; after which each company was brought forward and the men swore to observe the same. An order was then published that anyone harboring a Caesarian should produce him forthwith, and on their production all were publicly executed in the space outside the head quarters tent. Most of them, however, were secretly hidden by their hosts, and sent over the rampart during the night. But the result of this intimidation on the part of the leaders, and the infliction of this atrocious punishment upon our innocent men, taken in conjunction with the solemn obligation of the new oath, was to destroy all hopes of an immediate surrender, and, by changing the temper of the troops, to bring the situation once more back to the old arbitrament of war.

Meanwhile Caesar gave orders that such of his opponents' troops as had come across during the late period of negotiations should be collected together with every mark of respect, and sent back to their own camp. A certain proportion, however, of the group of officers and centurions preferred to stay with him, and were subsequently treated with conspicuous favor, the centurions being reappointed to their former companies, and all the officers who were Roman knights being gazetted according to their previous rank.

To revert now to the fortunes of the Afranians. Their foraging was exposed to constant attack, their watering conducted under the greatest difficulties. The legionaries amongst them possessed some small amount of supplies, having received orders to take rations for twenty-two days on quitting Lerida; but the Spanish infantry and native auxiliaries had none. Moreover, these last had but slender chances of obtaining any, and even if they did, were physically unequal to carrying heavy loads; consequently they deserted daily in large numbers to Caesar. It was beyond doubt a most critical position. Of the two plans open to them, the more advisable seemed to be a return to Lerida, where a small quantity of provisions had been left behind; for once there, they were confident of seeing their way through their subsequent difficulties. Tarragona was too far off, and over that distance of ground they were well aware that more than one accident might wreck their course. Having therefore settled on the former alternative, they marched out of their present entrenchments. Caesar at once detached his mounted men to harass and check their rearguard, whilst following in person with the legions; and without a moment's delay his cavalry became engaged with the tail of the Pompeian army.

The fighting that ensued proceeded along the following general lines. The rear of the retreating column was brought up by a number of infantry battalions, free of all superfluous baggage, and these, whenever the army's march lay through a plain, would be halted, several strong, to act as a covering force. Where a mountain range had to be scaled, the danger to this force was easily repelled simply by the nature of the ground, as the vanguard could use their higher position to protect their comrades toiling up the slope; but when a valley or other kind of descent lay before them, not only could the advanced party render no help to that which was checking the pursuit, but the Caesarian cavalry also, from their vantage-ground, rained down spears upon their backs, thereby gravely imperilling the safety of the force. The only way to meet this danger was, when they approached such places, to order the legions to halt, and by a determined charge scatter the enemy's horse; then, when these had been dislodged, the entire force would suddenly fling themselves down the hillside at the double, and, getting across the valley in this way, form up once more on the opposite heights. As for their own cavalry, so far were they from getting any help from it, though numerically a strong force, that, owing to its panic-stricken state consequent on the preceding engagements, it had itself to receive protection by being kept in the center of the column; and the invariable result of letting any trooper quit the line was to be instantly snapped up by the Caesarian horse.

Now when fighting of this nature is in progress, the march of an army is necessarily slow and tentative, involving frequent halts for the relief of its own units. And such was the case now. After proceeding four miles, the attacks of our cavalry became so galling, that the enemy were driven to seize a lofty hill; here they commenced fortifying one side of a camp where it faced their pursuers, though without unloading their baggage train. Subsequently, on seeing that Caesar's camp was fully laid out, with its tents pitched, and that his cavalry were absent with scattered foraging parties, they suddenly, about eleven o'clock on the same day, made a dash to escape; and, filled with a new hope of respite through the absence of the enemy's horse, started once more on the march. Aware of the new movement, Caesar first of all refreshed his troops, and then set out in pursuit; leaving behind one or two battalions to guard his baggage, and giving instructions that at four o'clock in the afternoon the foraging parties should follow and the cavalry be recalled. The latter force lost no time taking up their daily part in the march. Sharp fighting ensued along the rearguard, all but resulting in the enemy's rout, and involving several casualties amongst their rank and file and to some extent among their centurions.

Meanwhile Caesar was coming up, and his column, in full force, was now hard on their heels.

In this predicament, unable either to search for a suitable camping ground or to proceed further with their march, there remained no alternative but to halt, and to make a camp on a site both destitute of water and naturally unsuited to their purpose. Notwithstanding this, Caesar, acting on the reasons indicated above, refrained from all attack, and merely contented himself with not allowing any tents to be pitched after this day, in order that every man in his force might be the readier to take up the pursuit, no matter whether the enemy broke away by day or by night. The latter, on discovering the impracticable nature of their present site, employed all the hours of darkness in extending their lines, thus turning camp into camp; and this work was continued at daybreak on the following morning and occupied them throughout the ensuing day. Unfortunately, the further they carried their works and advanced their lines, the further they got from water; and they thus found themselves remedying their present evil only by incurring new ones. The first night after this no watering whatever was attempted; on the morrow a guard was left behind in camp, while the rest of the force moved out towards the watering place, though still not a single forager ventured to make his appearance. Caesar much preferred letting punishment of this kind do its work amongst them, and so force them to a surrender, to having to decide matters by a pitched battle. Yet, though this was so, it did not prevent him from attempting the circumvallation of his opponents by means of rampart and ditch; his object being to counteract as far as possible the surprise sorties which he foresaw they would be driven to adopt. It was with this design in view that on their side an order was now given to slaughter all baggage animals; a decision that under any circumstances would have been necessary, on account of their absolute dearth of fodder.

A period of two days was spent in arranging these works and the plans connected with them, and the third day found considerable progress made with much of the entrenchments. But about three o'clock in the afternoon of this day the enemy's signal for action suddenly sounded, and his legions, advancing from camp, drew up in line with the express object of preventing the completion of our fortifications. Caesar at once recalled his own regiments from his earthworks, ordered his cavalry to concentrate in force, and marshalled his line of battle. Thus much indeed was imperative on him; for to expose himself to the imputation of having shirked a contest, in face of the reasonable expectation of his troops and his general reputation with the world, would beyond all doubt have struck a serious blow at his prestige. On the other hand, he was still influenced by the reasons already indicated for not desiring a battle with his opponents, and even more so in the present instance, inasmuch as the narrow limits of the ground rendered it hardly possible to inflict a crushing defeat upon them, even if actually routed. For the space between the two camps did not exceed two miles; two-thirds of this was occupied by the rival armies, and the remainder just gave room enough to the troops for delivering their charge; consequently, in case of a general action, the defeated side would find an easy escape in its flight through the close proximity of its own camp. It was these considerations which had now determined him, whilst yet resisting any unprovoked attack, not himself to take the offensive.

The Afranians were in two lines, consisting of five Roman legions; whilst a third position in the rear was held by their native reserves. Caesar's army was in three lines; but his five legions were distributed with four battalions from each in the front line, then three more apiece as a first reserve, followed again by the same number once more, each battalion being always in support of part of its own legion. His archers and slingers were withdrawn inside the ranks of his center, whilst his two flanks were screened by cavalry. With their lines thus arranged, each party seemed to have attained its desired object: Caesar, to refuse battle unless forced upon it; the enemy, to hinder the construction of the other's earthworks. The situation, however, was only becoming prolonged; and the troops, after being kept in position till sunset, then parted from each other to their respective quarters.

The next day Caesar prepared to finish his incompleted works, whilst the Pompeians proceeded to try a ford over the Segre, in the hope of crossing that river. To frustrate this, Caesar threw his light-armed Germans with a cavalry section across the stream, along the banks of which he then posted a strong line of pickets.

Blockaded thus at every outlet, with what camp animals they still possessed now without fodder for four whole days, and destitute alike of water, fuel, and provisions, the Pompeian leaders at length petitioned to negotiate, and if possible, in some place at a distance from the troops. This last stipulation was refused by Caesar, who, however, agreed, if they so cared, to meet them in the open; whereupon the son of Afranius came over as a hostage, and the interview took place at a spot selected by Caesar. Here, in the ears of both armies, Afranius spoke as follows. "No blame attached, he hoped, either to himself, his colleague, or their army, for their natural desire to act loyally by Cneius Pompeius, their own commander. The claims of duty, however, had now been fully satisfied, and as to punishment, their complete destitution might well be regarded as adequate. They were now caged in virtually like wild beasts, debarred from water, and debarred from movement; and such a position was not physically more intolerable than it was galling to their pride. They accordingly confessed themselves beaten: at the same time they desired, if not too late, to make a strong appeal for mercy, in the hope that Caesar would not consider himself bound to exact from them the utmost penalty of war."

The whole speech, it should be added, was delivered with the greatest possible deference and respect.

In answer, Caesar reminded him that no man had ever had less justification than he to adopt a tone either of complaining of his lot, or of claiming commiseration for it.

> Everyone else had acted as became them: for himself, when he refused to force a conflict, though conditions were favorable and time and place to his own advantage; for his army, when they did not allow the outrage perpetrated on them by the murder of their comrades to deter them from preserving and guarding the lives of those in their power; finally, for Afranius' own men, by their taking the initiative in making overtures for peace, when they had even held it their duty to demand a safe-conduct for all their officers. Everyone, in short, had being animated by a spirit of conciliation; they, the leaders, had alone set their face against peace; they alone had disregarded the sanctity due to a time of *pourparlers* and of truce, and had foully butchered unsuspecting men, when duped by what they believed to be negotiations. They had met the fate that usually befell people of overweening obstinacy and pride; and now found themselves driven back upon, and even passionately desiring, a course which they lately regarded with contempt. However, he had no wish to use their present humiliation or to take advantage of the present opportunity in order to swell his own resources; but what he did insist upon was that those armies, which for so many years they had been nursing against himself, should now be disbanded He said "against himself," for no other explanation was possible of the dispatch of six legions to Spain, and the embodiment afterwards of a seventh raised in the Peninsula; or again of the mobilization of so many powerful fleets, and of the appointment of eminent soldiers to their command. Not one of these steps had

been necessary for the establishment of peace in the Spanish governments, or the normal military requirements of the
province; whose long unbroken rest made all reinforcements
superfluous. No, it was against himself that all these preparations had been for so long directed; it was to cripple him that
an unprecedented type of command was to be created, which
permitted a man to control the administration of the capital
from his residence outside the gates of Rome, and at the same
time to retain year after year the absentee governorship of two
provinces stocked with fighting races: it was solely to check-
mate himself that a violent change was now to be wrought in
the constitution of the magistracies, whereby governors were
sent out to provinces no longer, as before, at the expiration of
their consulship or praetorship, but upon the interested selec-
tion of a clique. Again, when he was to be opposed, no one was
allowed to plead the excuse of age; but veterans, well tried in
past campaigns, must be called out to take over the command
of the armies that were to crush him: and finally, in his case
only, an exception was made to the courtesy always extended
to all commanders alike, which allowed them, after success
in the field, to return home with honor, or at least not in disgrace, and there to disband their army. Yet all these insults he
had endured with patience, and would continue to endure;
nor was his object now to deprive them of their army in order
to retain it with his own, though doubtless that were an easy
matter; it was merely to disarm them of any weapon they could
afterwards turn against himself. That being so, he must, as
already indicated, call upon them to evacuate the provinces,
and to break up their army. Provided that were done, nobody
should suffer at his hands: that, however, was the one indispensable condition of peace.

Amongst the Afranian troops the notion that men, who justly
expected some sort of punishment, should actually be presented with
their discharge, was one affording high satisfaction and delight—as
indeed could be gathered from the way they now gave expression

to their feelings. For, on a question arising as to the time and place of carrying out this discharge, the whole army, from the position which they had taken up on the ramparts, began, with shouts and gesticulations, to declare that it must take place at once, and that, were it postponed, there would be no security of its afterwards being effected, no matter what pledge to the contrary might now be given. After a short discussion between the parties, it was finally arranged that all the men possessing house or property in Spain should receive their discharge on the spot, and the rest on arrival at the Var;[3] Caesar meanwhile giving a guarantee that no one should be molested, or compelled to take the military oath of allegiance to himself against his own personal inclinations.

He also took upon himself to find them in provisions from now onwards, during their march to the Var; and further added that, in the case of those who had lost property during the campaign, any of this now in the hands of his own troops should be restored to the losers, he himself compensating his men for everything, after fair valuation made.

Whatever subsequent disputes arose amongst the Pompeian soldiery were voluntarily brought to him for adjudication; and, upon a mutiny all but breaking out amongst the surrendered legions, owing to their clamoring for pay from Afranius and Petreius which the latter declared to be not yet due, a demand was made that Caesar should try the case; and his decision was at once accepted by both parties.

During the next two days about a third of the army received its discharge; after which Caesar gave orders for two of his own legions to start as an advanced guard, whilst the others followed close behind, thus ensuring that the two camps were not far apart. The whole operation was entrusted to one of his staff, Quintus Fufius Calenus; and, in accordance with the instructions issued to that officer, the army marched from Spain to the Var, and there the rest of the Pompeians were disbanded.

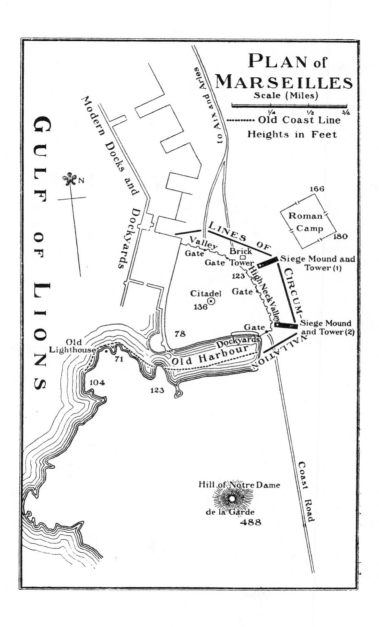

PLAN of
MARSEILLES

Scale (Miles)

¼   ½   ¾

.... Old Coast Line

Heights in Feet

GULF OF LIONS

Modern Docks and Dockyards

to Aix and Arles

N

166

Roman
Camp

180

LINES OF

Valley
Gate

Brick
Tower

Gate

Siege Mound and
Tower (1)

123

High Neck Valley

Gate

CIRCUM-

Citadel
136

78

Gate

Siege Mound
and Tower (2)

Old
Lighthouse

71

Old Harbour

Dockyards

CIRCUMVALLATION

104

123

Hill of Notre Dame
de la Garde
488

Coast Road

❧ BOOK II ❧

MARSEILLES
AND NORTH AFRICA

CHAPTER ONE

AN HISTORIC SIEGE

DURING THIS CAMPAIGN IN THE SPANISH PROVINCES, CAIUS Trebonius, the general left in charge of the assault on Marseilles (*Massilia*), had commenced operations by driving siege embankments against the wall of that city, surmounted by protection-sheds and wooden towers. One of these embankments was advanced on the side of the town close to the harbor and dockyards: the other by the gate where the road from Gaul and Spain enters the city, not far from the sea into which the river Rhone debouches. For Marseilles, it must be remembered, is washed by the sea on three sides of the town, the fourth alone offering a land approach; and even in this last section that part which faces the citadel is strongly protected by the natural conformation of the ground and by a deep ravine running under the wall, making an assault at this point a long and laborious process.

Trebonius, in order to carry out these works, now commandeered from the whole of Provence innumerable draft animals and day laborers, at the same time giving orders to accumulate large stores of osier wood and building-timber: then with these preparations completed, he proceeded to construct a siege mound eighty feet in height.

So great, however, was the original supply in the city of every species of war material, and so unlimited the number of siege guns, that none of the ordinary protection-sheds, constructed out of close-knit osier work, were found proof against the impact of their shot. Huge wooden harpoons, twelve feet long, and sheathed with a metal point, would be discharged with all the added impetus given by gigantic engines of war, and, tearing through four successive layers of hurdles, would bury themselves in the earth. The only remedy was to build a series of movable galleries, roofed with twelve-inch baulks firmly clamped together, under cover of which the workmen then found it possible to pass along the material from hand to hand. Ahead of the advancing mound, for the purpose of levelling all obstacles, moved a military tortoise, with a front of sixty feet, likewise built of stout timbers, and wrapped round with every kind of substance capable of withstanding the showers of fire and stones. Yet, in spite of these precautions, the vast scale of the works attempted, along with the great height of the enemy's wall and turrets, and the number of guns mounted on them, combined to render the progress of the operations everywhere a tedious one. Constant sallies, moreover, from the town were undertaken by the Albici, on which occasions fire would be freely flung upon the mound and towers: although indeed these attacks were always easily repulsed by our troops, who would even take the offensive and drive back the sortie parties into the town, with the infliction upon them of very considerable losses.

While the siege of the city was thus progressing, a movement towards its relief had been instituted by Pompeius, who had detached a squadron of sixteen warships, a few of them armed with copper-cased bows and ram, under the command of Lucius Nasidius, to sail to the assistance of Domitius and the Massilians. This officer made his way up the Sicilian Straits without the knowledge or suspicion of the acting governor Curio; and, putting in with his flotilla at Messina (*Messana*), took advantage of the flight of the leading citizens and local senators which followed on the sudden panic produced by his appearance, to launch one of their ships from the dockyards, and to incorporate it with the rest of his fleet. He then continued his voyage towards Marseilles, after secretly sending in advance a small dispatch vessel to apprise Domitius and the Massilians of his coming, and earnestly beg them once more to give battle to Brutus' squadron, now that they were reinforced by his own ships.

As a matter of fact, after their earlier reverse, the Massilians had drawn out of dockyard a number of old vessels equal to what they had lost, and had then proceeded with surprising energy to repair and fit these out. Their large reserves of oarsmen and skippers had also enabled them to supplement the fleet by several open fishing boats, which had been previously decked for the purpose of protecting the rowers from all exposure to spears; and the whole of these additional vessels were now given full complements both of archers and big guns. The squadron being by these methods at length fully equipped, the crews were incited by pathetic appeals from all the old men, matrons, and maidens of the city, not to fail their country in this her hour of need; after which they embarked with all the confidence and courage that had marked their first engagement. For it is a common weakness of human nature to be both unduly elated and alarmed in the face of the unseen and the unknown; and this law was now illustrated by the immoderate hopes and enthusiasm which the arrival of Lucius Nasidius had kindled in the Massilian republic.

Having secured a favorable wind, they put out from harbor, and effected a junction with Nasidius off Tarente (*Tauroenta*), a fortified settlement of Marseilles. Here they cleared their ships for action, heartened one another to face a second encounter, and arranged their respective duties in the approaching battle; it being agreed that the Massilians should form the right, and Nasidius the left division.

Meanwhile Brutus also bore down upon the same point, with a fleet considerably increased in numbers. His original twelve ships, built by Caesar's orders at Arles, had now been reinforced by the six lately captured from the Massilians, which during the intervening days he had repaired and made thoroughly efficient in every particular. After briefly encouraging his crews, therefore, to treat with contempt a beaten foe whose full strength they had already once vanquished, he moved out against them full of cheerful courage. From the camp of Trebonius and from all the higher ground in the vicinity[1] our investing forces easily overlooked the city, where they could see all the fighting population that had remained behind in the town, as well as all the older inhabitants, accompanied by wives and children and the city guard, either standing on the battlements with uplifted hands, or flocking to the temples of the eternal gods, before whose images they then prostrated themselves, praying heaven to grant them victory. Not a soul was there who did not realize that on the issue of this day hung the decision of all their future destiny. For those who had gone on board included young men from their best-known families, together with their most distinguished citizens in every period of life, all of whom had received a personal summons and earnest appeal for service. In case of disaster, therefore, they saw clearly that nothing would be left them afterwards even to try; while victory, on the other hand, whether gained by their own forces or by their foreign supports, would leave them confident in the ultimate success of their beloved city.

As soon as the action commenced, it became clear that the Massilians did not want for courage; but, remembering the commands lately laid upon them by their friends, they fought under the evident conviction that this was to be their last chance, and that those who ventured their lives in battle were only anticipating by a little the fate in store for the rest of their countrymen, all of whom must undergo the similar penalty of war upon the capture of their city. Accordingly, as our squadron slowly opened out, their commanders utilized the finer speed of their own ships for much skillful maneuvering; and, wherever we got an opportunity of throwing our grappling-irons and making fast one of their vessels, they would row up from every quarter to the help of their struggling consorts. Even here, at close quarters, they were formidable opponents, fighting, as they did, side by side with the Albici, and yielded little in courage to our own crews; whilst at the same time their smaller craft poured in a hail of spears at longer range, inflicting constant wounds without warning upon our hampered men. Two of their three-deckers[2] having sighted Brutus' flagship—easily recognizable by his pennant—had already set themselves in motion to ram her from opposite quarters, when the admiral, seeing his danger, put his vessel rapidly under way, and thus eluded them by the barest second. Advancing at high speed the two big ships crashed into one another with such terrific violence that both were badly crippled by the impact, whilst one had all her forepart carried away and became quite unmanageable. Seeing what had happened, the vessels of Brutus' fleet which were nearest to the spot dashed upon them in their difficulties, and quickly sent both to the bottom.

As to the squadron under Nasidius, it proved of no service whatever, and after a very brief interval withdrew out of action. These lacked the incentive of the sight of fatherland and the commands of dear ones to compel them to the utmost risk of life; consequently, from this division not a single ship was lost. The losses to the Massilian fleet, on the other hand, were five sunk, four captured, and one which fled with the ships of Nasidius, who all made for the coast of Eastern Spain. Of the surviving vessels one was sent on ahead to Marseilles to carry the news of the day's disaster; and whilst it was still approaching the city, the whole population streamed out to learn the issue of the fight; and on the truth becoming known, such a wail of lamentation ensued, that one might have thought the town had at that very moment been carried by assault.

Nevertheless, in spite of this defeat, the Massilians proceeded to complete their preparations for the defense of their city with the same dogged determination as before.

To resume the narrative of the landward operations. It was noticed by the legionaries in charge of the right, or northeastern, part of the siege-works, as a consequence of the repeated sorties of the enemy, that it would afford no little protection in that quarter, if, instead of a mere block-house to serve as a rallying-point, they were to build a full-sized brick tower, close under the city wall, where previously they had constructed only a small and low shelter against these same sudden attacks. It was to this shelter that they were in the habit of retiring; it was from this, moreover, that they fought as an advanced outpost, on the enemy pushing home any attack with unusual vigor; and it was out from this that they used to charge both to repulse and pursue him. Its dimensions were fully thirty feet square, but, on the other hand, its walls had been built five feet thick; and now, after its construction, in accordance with the law that experience is the universal guide in life, their applied intelligence led them to discover that the raising of this block-house to the height of a regular siege tower might prove of very considerable service. This transformation was effected as follows.

When the building had been raised high enough to carry a floor, the latter was carefully fitted into the outside walls in such a way that the heads of the beams, though extended into the brickwork, were nevertheless completely enclosed by the masonry, and thus prevented any protrusion outside on which fire flung by the defenders could lodge. Round this first floor were next piled pillars of small flat tiles, as high as the protection of the military screen and sheds they were using allowed of; and then, on the top of this temporary work, two large beams were laid, parallel with, and not far from the outer edge of, the two sidewalls—beams from which it was intended to hang the flooring that was to form the ultimate roof of the tower. Above these, and crossing them at right angles, joists were next laid down, and massed together by planking. These joists were made a little longer than the walls, and protruded beyond them, so that from their extremities could be suspended coverlets which should act as an impenetrable defense against all shots launched at the men whilst engaged upon that section of the wall which intervened between this roofing and the part already completed. The top of this floor was further paved with crude brick and mortar, to guard against any attempts of the enemy to damage it by fire; and, finally, a number of soaked cushions were thrown on, to prevent either the woodwork being broken by the discharges of artillery, or the brickwork smashed by the heavy shot from the mortars. Three large mats were next manufactured out of anchor hawsers, in length equal to the tower walls, and four feet deep; and these were then lashed to the protruding joists on the three sides exposed to the enemy, thereby forming a continuous curtain round the tower. These mats were made of this material, because experience elsewhere had proved it to be the only one capable of resisting the passage both of hand-spears and ordnance shot, no matter of what weight and size.

As soon as the already finished portion of the tower was thus covered and fortified against every sort of discharge from the enemy, the screens hitherto used were wheeled off to other parts of the siegeworks, and the men in the tower began to let the roof hang free and then to raise it with levers working from the first-floor beams; hoisting it as high as the suspension of the curtains allowed of. That done,

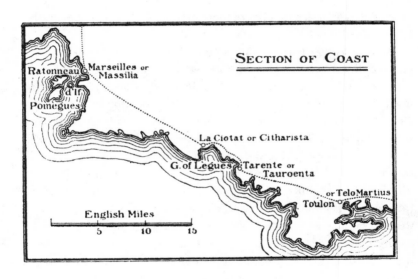

SECTION OF COAST

Ratonneau Marseilles or
            Massilia
    d'If
Pomegues

La Ciotat or Citharista

G. of Legues Tarente or
               Tauroenta

                or TeloMartius
         Toulon

English Miles
    5   10   15

they proceeded, completely hidden and protected by these coverings, to build up the four walls with brickwork; and, on the completion of this particular section, the overhanging hood was prised up anew, and a fresh space cleared for construction. When it was judged time for the insertion of the second floor, the beams were again fitted into and concealed by the outside layers of bricks; after which the new flooring was used, in its turn, as a leverage for once more hoisting the top roof-work and its hanging mats. In this way they effected the construction of altogether six stories, in perfect safety and without a wound or danger of any kind; leaving as they built, wherever occasion seemed to demand, a number of loopholes through which afterwards to direct artillery fire.

As soon as they felt confident that their position in the new tower enabled them to cover with its fire all the surrounding siege-buildings, they set to work to construct a sapping shelter, sixty feet in length, and made from timbers two feet square, with the intention of running it from the brick tower down to the enemy's wall and the particular bastion facing them. This shelter was of the following formation.

Two beams of equal length were first laid out upon the ground, four feet apart, into each of which was let a row of uprights five feet high. These were then coupled across by a series of strong braces, forming a slight angle in the center, on the top of which other beams were to be laid as a roof. Along these braces two-foot beams were accordingly fitted, and fastened by nails and metal clamps. The next step was to let in all along the edges of this roof, or, in other words, along the extremities of the beams which formed it, a raised ledge of wood, about three inches broad and high, for the purpose of holding the brickwork that was to follow. The frame having thus received an appropriate slant to its roof, and being neatly finished off, as soon as the roof beams were made fast upon the braces, the shed was cased above with crude brick, and mortar, as a protection against fire thrown from the battlements. These bricks were then given several coatings of stucco to prevent their being washed to pieces by water played upon them through pipes by the garrison: whilst, finally, the stucco itself was laid over with soaked cushions, to guard in turn against damage from either fire or heavy stones. The whole of this piece of work was kept hidden behind protection-sheds, and executed outside the tower itself: and, upon its completion, the legionaries, with a sudden movement totally unlocked for by the enemy, swept it out on rollers and, using a type of winch employed for beaching ships, rushed it down to the opposing bastion and fastened it to the masonry.

At the consternation wrought by this new peril the garrison fetched out crowbars, and, prising up the biggest stones that could be stirred, rolled them headlong down upon the sapping-shed. But its stout timbers held against the crash, and all that fell upon it slid off down the sloping roof. Seeing this, the enemy changed their tactics, and, filling barrels with pine shavings and pitch, set them alight and dropped them from the wall upon the shed below. These, as they struck the roof, also rolled to the ground, and were there fended off from the sides of the structure by means of long poles and pitchforks. Meanwhile, beneath the shelter, the troops were tearing out with crowbars the lowest stones of the enemy's tower holding the foundations together; during which operation the shed was guarded by the garrison of the brick tower, who poured in so hot a fire of hand-spears and artillery shot, that they drove the enemy from his wall and bastions, and thereby made it a harder task for him to withstand the progress of our sappers. Several stones had already been removed from the underground part of the bastion, when suddenly all that portion collapsed and fell, whilst the remainder looked like tottering to its fall.

At this, the enemy, unnerved by the sudden ruin of the tower, and overwhelmed by a reverse so unexpected, cowed also by the evident wrath of heaven, and dreading the plunder of their city, rushed out in a body through the gateway into the open, armed only with the white flag,[3] and with hands upraised towards the generals and the army, in token of surrender. Such an unexpected movement caused a complete suspension of military operations; and the soldiers ceased fighting, and eagerly turned to pick up what news they could. The enemy, on reaching the presence of the generals and the main army, threw themselves on their knees and begged to be allowed to await the arrival of Caesar. "They could see," so they declared, "that their city was now taken, that the Roman siege-works were completed, and their own bastion undermined: they accordingly gave up the defense. If, when Caesar arrived, they were to refuse compliance with his terms, he would only have to give the word, and nothing could possibly prevent the instant sacking of their town. Even as things were, they observed that, if the rest of the bastion went, it would be beyond the power of the Roman officers to restrain their men from bursting into the city in hopes of plunder, and levelling it with the ground."

All this, with much more to the same effect, was pleaded in tones of striking pathos and with a copious use of tears, as indeed was only to be expected from such past-masters of forensic eloquence.

Touched by this appeal, the Roman generals withdrew their forces from the siege ramparts, and abandoned the blockade, merely leaving a few sentinels upon the works. Humanity induced them to grant the enemy a sort of truce, while waiting the return of Caesar, and no further shot was fired either from the wall or from our own lines; but everybody, assuming the contest at an end, relaxed their precautions and vigilance. A further reason for the armistice was that Caesar had written strict injunctions to Trebonius not to allow the city to be taken by storm, lest the troops, who were unusually irritated at the town's revolt and its contemptuous defiance of their power, as well as by their own protracted exertions, should put the whole adult population to the sword, which indeed they threatened to do. Even now they were hardly to be restrained from breaking into the town, and were highly exasperated because they fancied that Trebonius had baulked them of their prey.

The enemy, however, were only faithlessly seeking a favorable opportunity for an act of most consummate treachery; and, after a few days' interval, when our men had to some extent grown slack and careless, they suddenly, about midday, whilst some of the guards were absent from their posts, and some weary after their long labors, actually asleep on the works, with all their accoutrements laid aside and in their covers,[4] burst out from the gates, and, aided by a strong wind, set fire to the siege buildings. The wind blew this fire in all directions, with the result that embankment and screens, tortoise, and wooden tower, together with the artillery upon it, simultaneously caught ablaze, and were all completely gutted before even the cause of the outbreak could be discovered.

Shaken by the sudden catastrophe, the troops who were on the spot seized what arms they could, and, others rushing up from the camp, a general attack was made upon the enemy. The latter indeed was quickly routed, but our men were prevented from pressing home the pursuit through the showers of arrows and artillery-shot launched upon them from the ramparts. The Massilians, on the other hand, fell back under the shelter of their walls, and there at their leisure proceeded to burn down both sapping-shed and brick tower. Thus disappeared in a few moments, through the enemy's treachery and the force of the gale, the accumulated work of many months. The same artifice was again attempted the next day, when, with the wind blowing as before, they charged out with even greater confidence to give battle at the second wooden tower and mound, dashing quantities of fire upon them. But, whereas on the first occasion our troops had completely relaxed their earlier vigilance of the siege; this time, warned by yesterday's mishap, they were found completely prepared for defense, with the consequence that the enemy was driven back into the town after heavy slaughter and the total failure of his plan.

Trebonius at once set himself to the task of taking in hand and rebuilding his ruined works, inspired by the greatly intensified enthusiasm of his troops. For on seeing the fiasco in which all their labors and preparations had now resulted, a wave of fury swept them at the thought of how their immense efforts would only look ridiculous in face of the fact that they were now totally destitute of even a source for obtaining further siege material, since every tree throughout the length and breadth of the Massilian territories had already been cut down and carted to the army. Accordingly they determined to substitute an unprecedented type of siege mound. This took the form of two parallel brick walls six feet each in width, roofed above, and of nearly equal height to the former embankment of timber. Wherever the space between the two, or the weakness of the material used seemed to require it, stout tie-rods were inserted as couplers, and big beams laid across to give additional strength; whilst every part of the roofing was covered with hurdle work, which, again, was coated with mortar. The men working below thus found themselves protected overhead by a roof, on each side by a wall, and in front by the shelter of a military screen, and could therefore safely bring up everything they wanted for the work. The enterprise was consequently carried through with expedition, and the lost fruits of their long labors were quickly regained by the ingenuity and devotion of the troops. Finally, gateways for future sorties were left at appropriate intervals in the wall.

The enemy thus saw the extensive buildings, whose reconstruction he had fondly hoped to be impossible, no matter what time were spent upon them, rebuilt with the labor and output of a few days, and rebuilt, moreover, in such a way as to leave no opening for any treacherous sally, or any possibility whatever either of injuring our troops by the discharge of spears or of damaging the works by fire. Simultaneously it came home to them that this first experiment might very well be so extended as to enclose the whole of the landward side of their city within a bastioned wall, which must then force them to abandon their position on their own fortifications, now that our troops had nearly effected a junction between their brick walls and those of the city, and were already throwing handspears. It was also clear that their big artillery, from which they had hoped so much, was rapidly becoming useless through the shortened range; and, each party having now equal opportunities of fighting from towers and battlements, they were quite conscious of their own inability to match our men in personal courage. It was these considerations which induced them to fall back once more upon the previous terms of capitulation.

CHAPTER TWO

THE CLEARING OF SOUTHERN SPAIN

MEANWHILE IN FURTHER OR WESTERN SPAIN, MARCUS VARRO HAD at first, upon news of the initial operations in Italy, given up the cause of Pompeius as lost, and continued to speak in the most flattering terms of Caesar. "Whilst his own interests," he declared, "were already engaged on the side of Pompeius, in virtue of the deputy-command he held from that leader, which bound him to the obligation of loyalty, his position was complicated by an equally strong friendship for Caesar. However, he knew what was the duty of a commander holding a commission of trust under a superior officer, and he knew too the forces at his own disposal, as well as the universal bias of his province towards Caesar."[1]

Such was the tone of all his conversation, reflected in his conduct by a general inactivity. Subsequently there came the information of Caesar's detention before Marseilles, of the junction of Petreius' forces with the army of Afranius, of the successful concentration of large bodies of auxiliaries, and the confident expectation of others equally strong, and, last but not least, of the unanimous feeling of the Eastern province for Pompeius. And when this was finally followed by the news of the critical state of Caesar's supplies before Lerida, communicated by Afranius in exaggerated and bombastic terms, he no longer hesitated to change his own attitude with the change of fortune.

Enlisting was organized throughout the province, till his two legions had been raised to their full complement and further strengthened by the addition of some thirty native battalions: he collected large supplies of corn, to be forwarded to the Massilians as well as to Afranius and Petreius; ordered the city of Cadiz (*Gades*) to build ten warships, whilst superintending the building of several more at Seville (*Hispalis*), and removed to Cadiz all money and valuables from the great temple of Hercules. From the province a force of six battalions was sent south to garrison Cadiz; Caius Gallonius, a Roman knight, and a friend of Domitius, who happened to be there on a business errand from the latter connected with a legacy, was installed as commandant of that town; and all arms, whether the property of the government or individuals, were ordered to be conveyed to the residence of the new governor.

These overt acts he followed up by delivering violent speeches against Caesar, and several times openly announced from his official platform that that commander had fought various unsuccessful actions, and that large bodies of his troops had gone over to Afranius; information of which he declared he had satisfied himself from most trustworthy messengers and indisputable sources.

Having by these methods terrorized the Roman citizens in his province, he coerced them into promising him for the public services £150,000 coin of the realm, and 20,000 pounds weight of bar silver, together with about 4,000 quarters of wheat: while, further to mark his bitterness, the townships suspected of sympathy with Caesar were saddled with the heaviest burdens, garrisons also being set up in their midst. Finally he allowed prosecutions to be brought against private individuals, by which any who had been guilty of treasonable language against the present regime had their goods confiscated to the state, and the entire province had to take an oath of allegiance to Pompeius and himself.

On learning the issue of the operations in Eastern Spain, he prepared for war, though the conduct of the war was to be a strange one, and consisted of retiring with his two legions upon Cadiz, and there locking up his fleet along with all his provisions; a course of action forced upon him by the discovery that his province was now solid for Caesar. There, on the island which forms that city, with sufficient ships and supplies of food, he regarded it an easy matter to effect the procrastination of the war.

Caesar, however, had determined, in spite of much urgent business which at this moment summoned him back to Italy, not to leave any area of war behind him in the Spanish provinces; for he was perfectly well aware of the signal benefits conferred by Pompeius upon the Eastern province, and of his immense following in that region.

He therefore dispatched the tribune Quintus Cassius[2] with a force of two legions to march upon Southern Spain, whilst he himself traveled ahead by rapid marches, and escorted by a bodyguard of six hundred horse. He also sent on before him a proclamation, fixing a date on which he desired the attendance at Cordova (*Corduba*) of the magistrates and leading citizens of all the communities in this part of the Peninsula. The terms of this proclamation were disseminated throughout the province; and, on the day appointed, there was not a single township which had not sent some members of its governing council to Cordova, and not a single Roman citizen of any standing who was not there to meet him.

During this time also the Roman settlement in Cordova took upon themselves to shut the city gates against Varro; guards and sentinels were posted upon the walls and turrets, and two of the so-called "colonial corps" having chanced to arrive there, they were kept under orders for the defense of the town. Simultaneously, the inhabitants of Carmona, by far the strongest township of the whole province, of their own initiative expelled the three battalions established in their citadel as a garrison by Varro, and then shut their gates against him.

All this only increased Varro's haste to get to Cadiz with his two legions as quickly as possible, lest he should find either the road or the passage across to the island barred in his face; so widespread and so decided did he now realize the feeling of the province to be in favor of Caesar. He had not gone far when dispatches met him from Cadiz informing him that the news of Caesar's manifesto had at once been followed by a conspiracy between the leaders of the town and the officers of the troops there in garrison, to eject Gallonius and hold the city and island for Caesar: that after the hatching of this plot an ultimatum had been addressed to Gallonius advising his voluntary departure from Cadiz, whilst he could safely do so (for otherwise the conspirators would take their own measures), and that upon this threat Gallonius had evacuated the town.

On hearing of this last development, one of the two legions, termed the home-born regiment,[3] pulled up from the ground its standards in Varro's camp, with their commander actually standing by and looking on, and then and there marched back to Seville; where, without committing any breach of discipline, it proceeded to bivouac in the market place and public colonnades of the city. This conduct won such warm approbation from the Roman citizens in that administrative area, that they each took some of the troops off to their own homes, and there entertained them with the keenest pleasure.

Proceedings like these caused Varro considerable misgiving. Changing his route, he started off with the hope of getting to Santiponce (*Italica*), only, however, to receive intelligence from his supporters that the gates were already closed against him. He was now cut off from every possible line of march, and, accordingly, sent in word to Caesar that he was prepared to surrender his remaining legion to whomever Caesar should direct him. The latter dispatched Sextus Caesar to his late opponent, bearing instructions for the legion to be surrendered to him. After the surrender, Varro came to meet Caesar at Cordova, where he gave a faithful return of all his government accounts, paying over whatever ready money he had in hand, and specifying all stores and ships anywhere under his immediate command.

Subsequently Caesar delivered a public address in a Durbar at Cordova, in which he expressed his gratitude to all the various classes of his audience in their order. First of all to the Roman citizens, for their active steps in securing the allegiance of the provincial capital; next to the Spaniards for their expulsion of the enemy's garrisons; then to the people of Cadiz, for successfully foiling the plots of his opponents and asserting their own independence of action; lastly to the officers and centurions, lately in garrison in that city, for having lent their military support to the execution of the policy of the civilians. After this, he released the Roman citizens from their undertaking to supply Varro with moneys for the public service; and at the same time restored their confiscated property to all who were proved to have been so fined for excessive freedom of speech.

Having then distinguished certain of his adherents by the grant of privileges both public and private in character, he filled the rest with bright hopes for their political future, and, after a stay of two days in Cordova, set out for Cadiz, where all treasure and valuables taken from the sanctuary of Hercules and afterwards lodged in a private dwelling-house were ordered to be restored to that temple. This done, he appointed Quintus Cassius as governor of the province with a military force of four legions; he then went on board the vessels lately built by Marcus Varro and, at his injunctions, by the town of Cadiz, and set sail for Tarragona (*Tarraco*), and, after a few days' voyage, cast anchor off that city. Here he found representatives of pretty well the whole Eastern province awaiting his arrival. Following the same policy as at Cordova, he selected certain communities to be the recipients of both public and personal distinctions, and afterwards left by the overland route for Narbonne, traveling thence on to Marseilles, where he learned that in accordance with a law passed by the people he had been nominated Dictator by Marcus Lepidus the praetor.

The Massilians he found reduced to the utmost straits. Their supplies were at starvation point, they had been twice beaten at sea, their numerous sallies had uniformly been repulsed, and now, to crown all, they were in the throes of a virulent plague. This last calamity was due to their long immurement and change of diet, the only food now obtainable being stale millet and moldy barley, stores of which grain had been long accumulated in public granaries as a provision against such contingencies. One of their bastion-towers was, moreover, down, and much of their wall undermined; whilst all hope had now disappeared of succor from the Spanish provinces and armies, the news of whose capture by Caesar had lately reached them. They therefore determined to surrender without further attempt at treachery. A few days, however, before the actual capitulation, Lucius Domitius, on discovering the intention of the town, had proceeded to fit out three ships; and, after allotting two of these to his suite, had himself embarked on the third; when, favored by dirty weather, he made a dash to escape. He was sighted by the vessels, which, by the orders of Brutus, lay daily off the harbor to enforce the blockade, and these

at once weighed anchor and gave chase. One of the three, viz. that
of Domitius, alone kept on her course, and continued her efforts to
escape, until, aided by the heavy weather, she was lost to sight by her
pursuers: the other two, frightened at seeing our warships closing in
upon them, put back into port.

The Massilians, in obedience to Caesar's orders, now brought out
through the town gates all the arms and siege-guns they possessed,
and then made over to Brutus all the ships remaining either in harbor or dockyards: simultaneously surrender was made of all funds in
the public Treasury. These preliminaries disposed of, Caesar agreed
to spare their autonomy, though more out of consideration, it must
be confessed, for the city's great name and distinguished history in
the past, than for any services they had rendered to himself. Leaving, therefore, a garrison of two legions in the place, he sent on the
remainder into Italy, and then started on his way to Rome.

→ CHAPTER THREE ←

THE SET-BACK IN AFRICA

IT WAS DURING THE EVENTS RECORDED IN THE PREVIOUS CHAPTER
that the expedition of Caius Curio to North Africa was begun and
ended. Exhibiting from the outset a fatal contempt for the military
strength of his opponent, Publius Attius Varus, he crossed over from
Sicily, accompanied by only two of the four legions originally given
him by Caesar, and by but five hundred cavalry; and, after a passage of some sixty hours, landed, on the morning of the third day,
at a place called Anquillaria. This spot is distant twenty-two miles
from Klibia (*Clupea*), and in summer-time offers a fairly convenient
anchorage, lying, as it does, between two bold headlands. Klibia itself
was occupied by the younger Lucius Caesar, who was cruising off the
port in readiness for Curio's arrival with a squadron of ten warships,
old vessels that had been hauled up into the dockyards of Utica at the
close of the war with the pirates, and fitted out again for the present
campaign by the orders of Attius. Their admiral had accordingly
taken alarm at the imposing numbers of our flotilla, and, flying from
the open sea, had run his flagship, a three-decker,[1] upon the nearest
point of the coastline, where he left it stranded, and set out overland
to the town of Susa (*Hadrumetum*), then held by a single legion under
Caius Considius Longus. The rest of the squadron, upon the flight of
their leader, likewise made for Susa. Meanwhile Curio's twelve warships, which he had brought over from Sicily to escort his transports,
started under the command of his paymaster Marcius Rufus and gave

chase to Caesar; but, on seeing the latter's vessel abandoned on the beach, they towed her off, and then returned to Curio.

The latter, after completing his disembarkation, directed Marcius to take the ships round to Utica, and, following their departure, set his army in motion for the same objective, a two days' march bringing him to the banks of the Medjerda (*Bagradas*). There leaving Caius Caninius Rebilus in charge of the legions, he rode forward with the cavalry to reconnoitre the old camp of Scipio,[2] a site which he believed to be admirably adapted for the permanent quarters of his army. It consists of a tongue of precipitous rock, jutting out into the sea, steep and rugged on two sides, but with a slightly less abrupt descent on that looking towards Utica, from which, by the direct route, it is little over a mile distant. This route, however, passes through springs, where there is a considerable inlet of the sea, converting all the surrounding district into a marsh, and anyone wishing to avoid this can only reach the town by a detour of fully six miles.

Having reconnoitred the position, Curio also succeeded in obtaining a view of his opponent's camp. It lay hard by the wall of the town, which it actually touched at what is known as the Military Gate. It thus had the advantage of great natural strength; for, in addition to the city of Utica itself forming one of its four sides, a second rested on the theater, which faces the town outside, and on the immensely strong substructures of this building; and lastly, the approach to it was both narrow and difficult of access.

Whilst investigating the camp, he noticed that all round the neighborhood the roads were thronged with the inhabitants carrying and driving loads of property from the country towards the city, hoping to convey it thither for safety in their panic at the sudden outbreak of war in their midst. Curio at once launched his cavalry upon this prospective plunder and booty; but had hardly given the word when a body of six hundred Numidian horse and four hundred foot emerged from the town, having been dispatched by Varus to act as an escort to the coveted prize. These troops had arrived at Utica a few days before as reinforcements from King Juba, whose action had been prompted, not merely by the old friendship between his father and Pompeius, but also by a feeling of intense animosity against Curio, who, in his tribunate of the year before, had laid a bill before the people, the ratification of which would have meant the annexation of Juba's kingdom. The opposing cavalry met in the shock of battle, but the opening charge was enough for the Numidians, who quite failed to stand their ground, and, with the loss of some 120 killed, fell back upon their camp outside the city wall. Meanwhile the warships had arrived off the town, and Curio at once ordered his admiral to notify the numerous fleet of merchantmen who lay off Utica some two hundred strong, that any captain who did not immediately bring his vessel round to the Cornelian camp would be regarded as an enemy. On receipt of this notice, the entire fleet, without a moment's hesitation, weighed anchor, and, leaving Utica, moved across to the place indicated, thereby enriching the army with abundant supplies of every description.

With this successful opening to the campaign, Curio returned to his camp on the Medjerda, and, as he rode in, was received by the thunderous applause of every man in his army, acclaiming him as their own victorious Commander.[3] The next day he moved with his force upon Utica, pitching his camp close by the city. The entrenchments of this were not yet completed, when his mounted pickets brought in word that large auxiliary bodies of horse and foot, dispatched by Juba, were approaching the town. Even as they spoke a heavy cloud of dust could be descried, and in another moment the head of the advancing column was in sight. Astounded at a sight so wholly unexpected, Curio threw forward his cavalry to hold back and check their advance, while he quickly recalled his infantry from the work of fortification, and arranged his line of battle. The cavalry dashed into action, and, before the legionaries could be deployed or assume their proper places in the ranks, it had swept back the king's forces in one confused mêlée; caught, as they were, in the same state of disorder and over-confidence as had characterized their march. A considerable portion of their infantry were cut to pieces; but nearly all the cavalry made good their escape by a headlong flight across the sands into the town.

During the night which followed this engagement two of Curio's centurions, Marsians[4] by birth, left his camp to desert to Attius Varus, taking with them twenty-two men of their two companies. Perhaps it

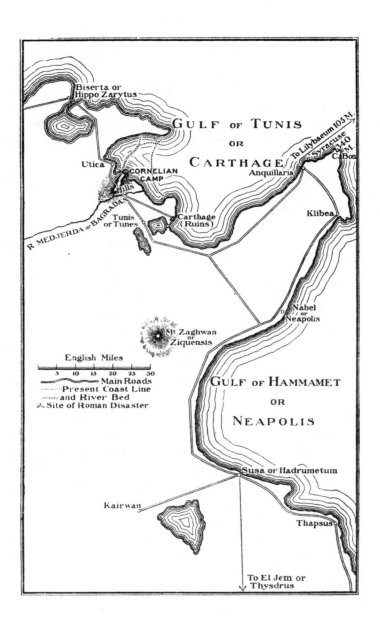

was their honest conviction that they reported to him, or perhaps it was only to declare themselves his courtiers as well as his soldiers— seeing that the wish is often father to the thought, and that our own opinions we would fain believe to be those of our neighbors—at all events they asserted disaffection to be rife in the army of Curio, and that the situation urgently demanded a meeting with his army which might give it an opportunity to negotiate. Their opinion weighed so much with Varus that early on the next morning he advanced his legions from camp: Curio immediately responded by a similar movement; and each commander then drew up his forces for battle, with merely a slight hollow separating the two hostile lines.

Now there was serving in the army of Varus, the Sextus Quintilius Varus who, as recorded above, had been one of those taken at Pentima (*Corfinium*). This officer, after being released by Caesar, had crossed to Africa; whilst Curio also, it will be remembered, had made up his expeditionary force out of the legions previously acquired by Caesar at the capture of Pentima. So closely, indeed, had their old organization been adhered to, that, with the exception of a few changes amongst the centurions, the personnel of the companies and battalions had undergone no change whatever. This fact now afforded Quintilius a pretext for addressing overtures to our men; and he accordingly proceeded to ride down the lines of Curio, appealing to the troops not to put lightly aside the recollection of their earlier oath of allegiance, sworn in the presence of Domitius and of himself as that general's paymaster, and not to bear arms against old comrades who had shared with them all the privations of a siege, nor to give their services to a party who only stigmatized them as traitors. He then wound up by hinting at the rewards which they might confidently expect from his own generosity in the event of their joining himself and Attius.

At the conclusion of the speech no indication whatever of their feeling was made on the part of Curio's army, whereupon both sides withdrew their forces to camp.

As soon as Curio's troops were back in their entrenchments a strange misgiving seized upon all ranks, and quickly gathered head as the various expressions of opinion made themselves heard. Exaggerated notions were conjured up by each man's private imagination, so that to the fears communicated by his comrades each also added something of his own. In this way an idea, which in reality emanated from a single individual, first spread its way amongst a few, and was then transmitted from man to man, until finally it appeared to rest upon the authority of quite a number. For, the reader must remember, it was a time of civil war, and one had to do with a class of men who possessed complete freedom of action, and could follow whatever course they chose. These legions again were peculiar in the fact that they had but recently been serving with those who were now ranged against them. Moreover, the very frequency of Caesar's leniency in dealing with surrendered foes had led them to underestimate his generosity. Some of the men, accordingly, now pressed for more decided action; others, inclined to temporize, could obtain but a cold hearing; and, finally, in some cases a fictitious air of defiance was assumed by those who wished to seem the bolder spirits.[5]

Such symptoms led Curio to summon a council of war to discuss the situation. On assembling, some of the officers were for going on at all hazards, and for actually storming the camp of Varus; holding that, where troops were contemplating measures of this nature, the most fatal thing of all was inaction; and, come what might, it was better to try the fortune of battle with sword in hand than to be deserted and betrayed by their own men, and afterwards have to undergo the extreme penalty of war. Others were of opinion they should fall back in the early hours of the morning upon the old camp of Scipio, so that the men might recover their senses after being kept a few days longer from all contact with the enemy; pointing out also that, in the case of disaster, the large number of ships lying there would give them a safer and easier retreat back to Sicily than that afforded by their present position.

Neither plan commended itself to Curio, who considered one scheme to err as much by defect of courage as the other did by excess, when half of those present looked favorably upon what was nothing less than the most cowardly flight, and the other half were for giving battle even with the advantage of position directly against them. For what sort of confidence was it that led anyone to believe in the possibility of storming a camp, defended, not merely by artificial, but also by immense natural fortifications? And how were they the better off if, after a crushing defeat, they were compelled to fall back from the assault? Surely it was a well-established axiom that while success in the field ensured for commanders the devotion of their troops, disaster no less earned their hatred. Then, as to the proposal to change their own quarters, he could see in it nothing but an ignominious flight, prompted by unmitigated despair, and inevitably to be followed by the disaffection of the army. Their plain interests demanded that no handle should be given, either to the men who were loyal, to suspect that their allegiance was doubted, or to the mutineers, to discover the dread which they inspired; for any signs of wavering on their own part not only strengthened the insubordination of the disaffected, but also weakened the obedience of the well disposed. Granted, therefore, that they were really satisfied of the substantial truth of the reports concerning the army's disloyalty—which he, for his part, felt confident were either pure fabrications or at any rate less serious than was generally supposed—how much more dignified a course was it to ignore such rumors and to keep them secret, rather than allow their own conduct to be taken as their confirmation? Every man when engaged in battle endeavored to conceal his own wounds: ought they not similarly to cover up the weak places in an army, which might otherwise tend to raise their adversaries' hopes? If he were told that these dangers were discounted by the proposal to march at midnight, all he could say was that such a proposal, in his opinion, put a direct premium upon any leanings towards misconduct. Movements of this character were only restrained by one of two incentives, either feelings of honor or fear of punishment, and both these checks were least operative at night. To sum up therefore. He was neither such a fire-eater as to urge a hopeless attack upon fortified entrenchments, nor such a poltroon as to throw up the expedition in despair. On the contrary, he was of the opinion that every other alternative should first be tried, and he already felt confident that he should carry the great majority of the council with him in this decision.

Having dismissed his council, Curio summoned a general meeting of the troops. On their assembly, he recalled to their recollection the enthusiastic devotion they had tendered Caesar at Pentima, and reminded them how their friendly initiative at that time had put a large part of Italy at his feet.

"One after the other," he continued,

> . . . all the country towns followed your guidance and repeated your action; and well might Caesar then regard your decision with feelings of profoundest gratitude, and the Pompeians with those of dismay. For mark the consequences. In the camp of the enemy that first verdict of yours told so heavily, that, without any defeat in a pitched battle, Pompeius ordered the evacuation of Italy; whilst Caesar, to show his trust in you, at once committed to your safeguarding one of his dearest friends in the person of myself, along with the government of Sicily and North Africa; countries whose resources are indispensable to him if he is to retain the capital and Italy.[6] But, I am reminded, there are some who would now urge you to leave us. It may well be so. For what could afford them keener pleasure than to outmaneuver us and at the same time to involve you in a piece of low villany; or what grosser insult to yourselves can their impotent rage suggest, than that you should betray the party which attributes its success solely to your attitude, and walk into the arms of those who hold you responsible for all their disasters? You surely have heard of Caesar's triumphant career in Spain, and how two armies, with their two commanders, have gone down before him, and two provinces been brought under his control; and that all this has been accomplished within forty days of his first sighting his opponents. Is it conceivable that a side which could make no stand with all its forces intact can now do so when its cause is lost; and can you, who declared for Caesar when victory still hung in the balance, now think of siding with the vanquished, after the issue of the war is decided, and when you ought to be reaping the reward of your services? But perhaps you feel uneasy at what they allege to have been your desertion and betrayal of their cause, and at their reference to your earlier oath of allegiance. Well, I ask you, was it you who deserted Lucius Domitius, or was it he who abandoned

you? Is it not the fact that he threw you over when you were fully prepared to go on to the bitter end, and that he tried to save his own skin without a single word to yourselves? And is it not equally true that after being betrayed by him you received back your lives as the free gift of Caesar? So much then for the alleged desertion; and as to the oath, what authority had he to hold you to it, when the insignia of his office[7] had been surrendered, his military command laid down, and he himself had passed under the higher authority of his captor, becoming a mere prisoner of war and a magistrate no longer? It is indeed a queer notion of a soldier's obligation they are left to appeal to, if they think it incumbent upon you to disregard the oath by which you are at present bound, in order to reconsider that which expired by the capitulation of the general who dictated it, and by the forfeiture of his legal standing which that capitulation involved.

Possibly, however, I am to conclude that, though you approve of Caesar, you find fault with me. I am not now going to talk about my own claims upon your gratitude, which still fall short of what either I could wish or yourselves expect; but let me remind you it is always at the end of a war that soldiers look for the reward of their efforts, and what that end is going to be not even you can doubt. Yet why should I not mention the great care we have shown for your safety, as well as the success that has so far attended our expedition? Do you regret that I brought the whole army over in perfect safety without the loss of a single transport? That on my arrival I scattered the enemy's fleet at the first encounter? That in two successive days I won two cavalry engagements? That I secured for us out of the harbor and bay occupied by the enemy two hundred laden merchantmen, and forced him into a position where no provisions could reach him either overland or by sea? However, if you will, fling away good fortune such as this, and leaders with this record, and go and identify yourselves with the disgraceful fiasco of Pentima, the ignominious flight from Italy, and the surrender of the Spanish provinces—all of them a sure forecast of the verdict on this African war. For myself, I was always content to be called a soldier of Caesar, and it was you who acclaimed me by the title of Commander. If you regret it, I return you your gift; but do you at the same time give me back my former name, unless you wish the honor you then bestowed upon me to be taken as a deliberate insult to myself.

Such a speech aroused the deepest feelings of the soldiery; and even during its delivery constant interruptions were heard, showing that the suspicion of disloyalty stirred them to an almost intolerable indignation. On his leaving the assembly they swarmed around him, and with one voice bade him dismiss his doubts, and not hesitate at any moment to give battle to the enemy, and so put their loyalty and resolution to the test. This demonstration of the men's feeling completely altered both the temper and mental attitude of the whole army, and Curio resolved accordingly, with the approval of his staff, to risk a decisive action upon the first opportunity that offered. On the morrow, therefore, he moved out from his lines and drew up for battle on the position occupied by his troops during each of the preceding days. Equally little did Attius Varus pause to consider before advancing his own force, determined as he was to profit by any occasion that might present itself either of tampering with his opponent's army or of engaging it on equal terms.

As already indicated, the two embattled lines were separated by a ravine, of no great size, but presenting a steep and difficult ascent. Each commander, therefore, maneuvering for the better position delayed his attack in the hope that his adversary would attempt the passage of this donga. After some interval, a movement was observed on the left wing of Attius, where, it was noticed, the full strength of his cavalry, together with a large contingent of Numidian light infantry interspersed through its ranks, was descending the banks of the ravine. To meet this attack Curio dispatched his cavalry and two battalions of Marrucinians[8]; but the enemy's squadrons refused to face the charge, and, stretching their horses to the gallop, hastened back to their main body; whereupon the light infantry who had accompanied the forward movement were, through this desertion by the cavalry, in course of being surrounded and cut to pieces by our troops. On this point were now concentrated the eyes of the whole Pompeian line, as they watched the flight and slaughter of their comrades; and it was at this critical moment that Rebilus, one of Caesar's generals, whose wide military experience had led Curio to bring him over from Sicily with the expedition, turned to his commander, and pointing to the confusion among the enemy, asked why he hesitated to seize the opportunity thus offered. With a single word to his troops to remember their promises of the previous day, Curio put himself at their head, and ordered them to follow. On reaching the ravine they were met by such formidable obstacles at its ascent, that the leading files, when not shouldered up behind by their comrades, only clambered out with the greatest exertions. But the legionaries of Atius had no stomach for a fight, as the sight of the recent flight and massacre of their auxiliaries had left them paralysed with terror, and their imagination already represented them as surrounded by our cavalry. The result was, that before a single javelin could be thrown, or our men get to closer quarters, the whole of the enemy's line turned and broke, retreating in confusion upon their camp.

In the pursuit which followed a soldier named Fabius, a Pelignian[9] by race, and a centurion in one of the inferior companies of his legion, worked his way to the head of the flying enemy, continually shouting the name of Varus, and searching for him everywhere, thus giving the impression that he was one of his own men and had something of importance to communicate. That general, on hearing himself so often addressed, looked at the man and stopped to ask him who he was and what he wanted. In a moment the other had raised his sword and slashed at the officer's unguarded shoulder, and was within an ace of killing him, had not Varus brought his shield up to parry the blow and so escaped with his life. Fabius was thereupon immediately surrounded and cut down by the bystanders.

When the flying rout approached the camp, the gates quickly became blocked and the road jammed with the crowded rabble, and the losses here incurred without the infliction of any wound were even heavier than during either the action or the pursuit. At one time it looked as if the enemy would actually be driven from his entrenched camp; and, indeed, some of the fugitives only halted upon reaching the shelter of the town. The natural advantage of its position, however, and the strength of its fortifications, effectually barred all approach: and it was further rendered impracticable by the want of the proper tools and appliances, since our men had left camp equipped only for a pitched battle and not for an assault upon fortified entrenchments. Curio, therefore, withdrew his army back to his own lines, with the single loss of Fabius, in contrast with the six hundred killed and one thousand wounded on the side of his opponent. After his retirement, all the enemy's wounded, and many more whose fears had since developed imaginary wounds, left the camp and made their way into the town. The discovery of this fraud, and the knowledge that his army was demoralized with panic, made active measures on the part of Varus imperative. Giving orders, therefore, for a single bugler and a certain number of tents to be left behind to disarm suspicion, he struck camp in silence[10] during the early hours of morning, and moved into the city with all his army.

On the following day Curio commenced the siege and blockade of Utica. The composition of this town was peculiar. Long years of quiet ease had made its crowded populace unfamiliar with war: old services rendered by Caesar had made the body of burgesses his friends: the Roman settlement in the city was distinctly heterogeneous in character: finally, over all alike was the terror inspired by the result of preceding battles. It was no wonder, then, that open suggestions for capitulation already made themselves heard in all quarters, and a petition was laid before Varus demanding the sacrifice of his own *amor propre* to the threatened ruin of the whole community. In the midst of these negotiations couriers arrived from King Juba, charged with the announcement that that monarch was close at hand at the head of a strong relieving force, and begging the inhabitants to take every step for the retention and defense of the town. This intelligence restored the hopes of the panic-stricken city; but Curio for sometime refused to give it any credence, so confident was he of his own security. In this attitude he was still further strengthened by the fact that authentic news of Caesar's victories in Spain was now beginning to reach Africa; and all these circumstances combined to embolden him to the supposition that the king would take no overt measures against him. The subsequent intelligence, however, from indisputable sources that the Numidian host was now less than twenty-five miles from Utica, determined him to abandon his siege-works, and to fall back upon the old camp of Scipio.

Here he proceeded to collect supplies of grain, to superintend the fortification of his lines, and to lay in stocks of fuel; urgent orders being meanwhile sent across to Sicily for the dispatch of his two remaining legions and the rest of the cavalry. The camp itself was admirably adapted for the delay of operations. Not only was the natural strength of its position still further increased by intrench-ments, but it rested on the proximity of the sea, and could also reckon on an abundance of fresh water and cooking-salt, large quantities of which had already been conveyed into it from the salt-pans of the neighborhood. There was no fear, either, of their fuel giving out, tim-ber being everywhere plentiful, nor of their corn, as the fields around were laden with it. Thus with the approval of his staff, Curio prepared to await reinforcements, and to prolong the course of the campaign.

Scarcely had these dispositions been made and these plans agreed upon, when word was brought in by a party of deserters from the townspeople that Juba had been summoned back by the outbreak of a frontier war and a quarrel with the city of Leptis; that this had caused his own detention at home, whilst his lieutenant Saburra had been dispatched at the head of a merely nominal force, and was now advancing upon Utica. An over hasty acceptance of these state-ments led to a fatal modification of Curio's original scheme, and he now determined to bring matters to the issue of a pitched battle. Among the causes which specially predisposed him to the adoption of this decision was, first of all, the impulsiveness of youth, combined with a high degree of native courage; to which must be added the stimulus of previous success, and an absolute confidence of coming victory. Fired by these incentives, he sent off the whole of his cavalry at nightfall, with instructions to attack the enemy's camp on the Medjerda; and there, no doubt, as his previous intelligence indicated, Saburra was in command. What he did not know was that the Numid-ian king was following in the rear of his lieutenant, and lay that night encamped only six miles behind him. The cavalry completed their march while it was still dark, and fell upon the enemy before these had any knowledge or suspicion of their presence. With what seems to be a tradition among foreign nations, the African force lay scattered about their camping-ground without any properly made lines; consequently, when our troopers dashed in upon the broken groups of heavily sleeping men, numbers were slaughtered on the spot, and a considerable body took refuge in panic-stricken flight. Their object thus attained, the squadrons set out on their return journey to Curio, taking their prisoners along with them.

Meanwhile Curio with the infantry had marched about an hour before dawn, taking with him the whole of his effective force, except five battalions which were left behind to garrison the camp. After going six miles he met his returning cavalry, who reported to him their recent action. A question to the prisoners elicited the answer that Saburra had been in command of the camp on the Medjerda (*Bagradas*): the rest of the facts he omitted to investigate, in his eagerness to get to the end of his march. Looking round at his leading files, "You see, men," he exclaimed, "how the prisoners' tale tallies with that of the deserters. The king is not here, and only a weak force has been sent, who were not even a match for a few squadrons of horse. On then, on then to the spoil, on to fame and glory, so that at last we may begin to think how we can best reward you, and how best acknowledge your services."

Now it was no mean performance that the cavalry had accomplished, particularly if their insignificant numbers were compared with the host of the Numidians; but, even as people always love to sound their own praises, the men, not content with this, began vaunting their achievements. Moreover, the eye fell upon a quantity of booty that the column had in train, and amongst the captures could be seen a number of men and horses, so that every moment lost seemed an unnecessary postponement of victory. The great expectations of Curio, therefore, were amply seconded by the excitement of his men. The cavalry were ordered to turn once more, and the pace of the march was quickened, in order that the enemy might be attacked at the height of the panic produced by their recent flight.

But the task was beyond them; horse and rider were both spent by the hard work of a whole night's march, and one after the other they dropped out of the column. Even this warning failed to check the ardor of Curio.

In the meantime Juba had been informed by Saburra of the night engagement, and at once pushed up to his support a force of two thousand Spanish and Gallic horse, which constituted his permanent bodyguard, together with the most trustworthy portion of his infantry. These were followed more leisurely by the king himself with the remainder of his army, including sixty elephants. Having taken these precautions, Saburra, suspecting that the advance of the Roman cavalry meant the near approach of the Roman general also, drew up his contingents of horse and foot with orders, upon the advance of the enemy, to simulate panic and gradually give ground and fall back, promising at the right moment to give them the signal for battle together with their necessary instructions for action. The situation, therefore, which presented itself to Curio upon his arrival on the scene only tended to confirm his already extravagant hopes; and, under the belief that the Numidians were in genuine flight, he left the shelter of the surrounding heights and began a descent into the plain.

The hills had been left behind some considerable distance when the utter exhaustion of the army, produced by the severity of a march of fully sixteen miles, at length compelled a halt. Then at last Saburra gave his signal, settled his line of battle and, riding down the ranks, proceeded to harangue his tribesmen. Only his horse, however, were placed in the fighting line; all his unmounted troops being stationed some little distance apart, to produce merely a moral effect by their imposing numbers. Nor was Curio less anxious for battle, but with words of cheer to his soldiers urged upon them to trust only to their own right arms. The infantry of the legions, in spite of their exhaustion, were eager for the fray, and fought with all their accustomed valor, as also did the handful of toil-spent cavalry; though these last now counted but two hundred sabres, the rest having all fallen out on the march. Nevertheless, weakened as they were, they forced back the enemy's line at whatever point they charged, but they had not the strength either to follow up the retreating horsemen, or to spur their own jaded horses to a quicker pace. The enemy, on the other hand, presently commenced a movement to envelope our whole line, one division of horsemen starting from each flank and working forwards to meet the other, thereby endeavoring to ride our men down from the rear. To prevent this, a few battalions would every now and again make a sally from the main body, but the rapid movement of the Numidians always enabled them to elude the charge; and as our men once more fell back upon their supports, they would wheel and attempt to surround them, and cut off their retreat from the rest of the line. Thus there was no way of safety for the Roman force either in standing their ground and preserving their formation, or by taking their chance in a desperate charge. Moreover, the enemy's numbers were continually increasing by reinforcements forwarded by the king, whilst the strength of our own men was steadily failing through fatigue. An intensification of their sufferings was the impossibility of attending to the wounded, who could neither leave the fighting line, nor be carried to a place of safety, since the whole of our position was effectually commanded by the enemy's encircling squadrons. Resigning, therefore, all hope of escape, they began to give way to those bitter outcries against death which man generally utters in his last hour, or else they turned to their comrades and begged them to look to their aged parents at home, if Fate should enable any of them to survive the disasters of that day. On all sides was panic and despair.

Seeing the state of universal terror pervading his troops, and that they were deaf alike to exhortation and entreaty, Curio, as a last hope in a piteous situation, ordered all ranks to take to the nearest hills, and the whole army to advance in line upon them. But even this outlet was forestalled by Saburra, who detached a body of horsemen to seize it in advance. This last disappointment gave the crowning touch to their despair. Some broke and fled, but were caught and cut in pieces by the pursuing cavalry; others simply went down as they stood. An appeal was made to Curio by his cavalry brigadier, Cneius Domitius, who closed round him with a few of his troopers, begging him seek safety in flight and make a dash for the camp, and promising not to leave his side. But Curio answered unhesitatingly that, having lost the army which Caesar had entrusted to his charge, he would never go back to look him in the face, and with that answer he died fighting. Only a very small proportion of the Roman cavalry escaped from the battle; but those who, as recorded above, had dropped behind in the rear for the purpose of resting their horses, on observing from their distant position that the whole army was a rout, made good their return to the camp. The infantry were all cut down to a man.

In the camp Curio's paymaster, Marcius Rufus, had been left in command; and, on receiving news of the disaster, that officer at once used all his efforts with the garrison to face their critical situation with calmness. Their only answer was a clamorous demand to be taken back to Sicily on board the ships. To this he consented, and gave orders to the shipmasters to have all boats down at the beach directly it was dark. So unrestrained, however, was the universal panic, that the wildest rumors went afloat. Some said that Juba's forces were outside the gates; others declared that Varus was marching upon them with his two legions, and that they already distinguished the dust of his approach—both statements being equally devoid of truth; whilst others, again, anticipated that the enemy's fleet would swoop down upon them without delay. In this state of abject terror every man looked to himself. The crews of the fleet of warships made all haste to depart, and the example of their flight had such a bad effect upon the merchant skippers, that only a few small dinghies responded to the call of duty and the previously issued instructions. Even then so fierce was the struggle along the crowded beach as to who should get first on board out of all the dense multitude, that some of the boats were swamped by sheer weight of numbers, while the rest hesitated to come in nearer, through fear of encountering a similar fate.

The end of the matter was that a few soldiers and a certain number of civilian residents, whose popularity or powers of appeal were exceptional, or who contrived to swim out to the ships, were received on board and taken safely across to Sicily: the rest of the force sent its centurions that night to Varus to act as plenipotentiaries, and surrendered themselves into that officer's hands. The next day Juba arrived, and outside the town his eye falling upon the men of the surrendered battalions, he boastfully claimed them as his own booty, and immediately ordered off to execution the large majority, though a few were reserved to be sent away for captivity into his own dominions; Varus all the while protesting against this violation of his sworn promise, yet not venturing to oppose it.

The African king subsequently entered the town on horseback with a large number of Roman senators in his train, amongst whom could be seen Servius Sulpicius and Licinius Damasippus. There he made what arrangements pleased him, giving orders to a small number of adherents as to his wishes with regard to Utica; and then, after a few days more, returned to his own kingdom, taking along with him the whole of his military forces.

❦ BOOK III ❧

DYRRACHIUM AND PHARSALIA

THE PASSAGE OF THE ADRIATIC

THE ELECTIONS WHICH WERE HELD IN THE AUTUMN UNDER THE presidency of Caesar, by virtue of his dictatorial powers, resulted in the return of himself and Publius Servilius as the consuls for the ensuing year; that being the year in which the law of the constitution again allowed Caesar to hold the consulship.[1] The electoral business disposed of, his attention was next demanded by the insecurity of public credit throughout the country, which was already producing a disinclination to the discharge of legitimate liabilities. He accordingly appointed a board of arbitrators with powers to make a valuation of all property, both real and personal, on the basis of its money value before the outbreak of the war; and, upon their estimate, the property was then to be transferred to creditors as legal tender. This measure he considered most nearly designed to effect the twofold purpose of at once removing and modifying those fears of a general repudiation of debts which foreign wars and civil disturbances tend to create, as well as of maintaining intact the social position of debtors.

With a similar policy, he also provided for a series of public resolutions to be laid before the assembled populace by the praetors and people's tribunes, restoring to their full civic rights certain of those who had been convicted under the Pompeian law relating to bribery. These men had been tried during the recent years when Pompeius had garrisoned Rome with strong detachments from his legions; and under that intimidation each trial had been finished off in a single day, with a different body of jurymen to hear the evidence from that which gave the verdict. These exiles had tendered Caesar their support at the opening of the present war, in the event of his caring to avail himself of their military services; and this spontaneous offer on their part he now regarded as equivalent to his having actually profited by it. The particular method adopted in their restoration arose out of deference to constituted usage, which demanded that their return should be effected by a formal and judicial expression of the popular will, rather than look like a private act of clemency of his own. By taking this course he avoided not only the charge of want of gratitude in repaying past services to himself, but also any suspicion of arrogance in usurping the people's constitutional right of granting privilege.

These measures, along with the Latin Festival[2] and the transaction of all outstanding comitial business, took up altogether eleven days; after that, Caesar laid down his dictatorship, and, taking his departure from the capital,[3] traveled through to Brindisi. Orders had already been issued for the concentration there of twelve legions of infantry and all his cavalry; though on arrival he found the transports assembled were barely sufficient to carry over fifteen thousand legionaries with five hundred mounted troops. (It was this want of troopships it should be noted that constituted for Caesar the sole obstacle to a rapid termination of the war.) Moreover, the forces actually available had to embark at something far below their normal strength. The long series of Gallic wars had made large gaps in their ranks; their numbers had further been greatly reduced by the protracted overland march from Spain; whilst the pestilential moisture of an autumn spent in Apulia and round the neighborhood of Brindisi, following after the exceptionally healthy regions of Gaul and Spain, had produced an outbreak of sickness through, the whole army.

Very different were the circumstances of Pompeius. Having secured a full year's period for the mobilization of his forces, a period undisturbed by war and unhampered by the presence of an enemy, he had used the respite in collecting an enormous fleet[4] from Asia Minor and the Cyclades, from Corfu (*Corcyra*), Athens, Pontus, Bithynia, Syria, Cilicia, Phoenicia, and Egypt, and had further taken steps to construct another of equal magnitude in all the maritime ports. He had likewise levied enormous sums of ready money upon the provinces of Asia Minor and Syria, upon the various eastern kings, potentates, and petty sovereigns, and upon the self-governing states of Greece; and not content with this, he had obliged the large commercial houses, which farmed the public revenues in the provinces under his military control, to pay over to him another equally enormous contribution.

As to his land forces, nine legions of Roman citizens had in all been got together. These included, first of all, the five brought over from Italy; in addition, a sixth drawn from Cilicia, which, owing to its formation out of two others, he called the Twin Regiment; another raised in Crete and Macedonia among the veterans settled in these provinces after their discharge by former commanders; and lastly two that had arrived from Asia Minor, where they had been lately embodied by order of the consul Lentulus. Besides this infantry of the line, large contingents had been called for from Thessaly, Boeotia, the Peloponnese, and Epirus, to be distributed among the legions by way of supplementary drafts, a treatment likewise extended to the surrendered troops of Caius Antonius;[5] whilst finally, to complete his regular forces, he was expecting two more legions from Syria, which were now advancing under their commander Scipio.[6] His irregular corps included three thousand archers, drawn from Crete, Sparta, Pontus, Syria, and all other states that could furnish them; as well as two battalions of slingers, each six hundred strong. His cavalry mustered seven thousand sabres, and was composed of the following contingents. From Galatia Deiotarus had brought six hundred Gallic horsemen, and Ariobarzanes five hundred from Cappadocia; and a like number was contributed from Thrace by Cotys, who had also sent his son Sadala. From Macedonia came two hundred troopers under Rhascypolis, a brilliant soldier; while a force of five hundred Gauls and Germans had been shipped from Alexandria with the Egyptian fleet by the younger Pompeius, forming a detachment of the Gabinian troops lately left behind in that city by Aulus Gabinius as a protecting garrison to King Ptolemy.[7] Another eight hundred had been enrolled from Pompeius' own slaves and herdsmen; three hundred had been provided from Gallograecia by Tarcondarius Castor and Domnilaus—the former coming in person with his force, the latter sending his son; and two hundred more had been dispatched from Syria by Antiochus of Commagene—handsomely rewarded for it by Pompeius—the majority of whom consisted of mounted archers. To these contingents were added bodies of Dardanians and Bessians, partly mercenaries, partly enrolled by military order or through personal influence, in conjunction with similar bodies of Macedonians, Thessalians, and various other tribes and townships, bringing up the grand total to the figure already mentioned.

Immense stores of provisions had been accumulated from Thessaly, Asia Minor, Egypt, Crete, Greece, and other districts: and Pompeius had now determined to winter at Durazzo (*Dyrrachium*), Apollonia, and the other maritime towns, with the object of preventing the passage of the Adriatic by Caesar; for which purpose also the fleet had been strung out along the whole of the Illyrian coastline. This fleet was in several detachments. The Egyptian squadron was commanded by the younger Pompeius, that of Asia Minor by Decimus Laelius and Caius Triarius, that of Syria by Caius Cassius, the Rhodian by Caius Marcellus, who had Caius Coponius as a colleague, and the Liburnian and Greek by Scribonias Libo and Marcus Octavius. The naval service as a whole, however, was under the supervision of Marcus Bibulus, who directed all the operations, and the supreme command rested with that officer.

To return now to Caesar. On arrival at Brindisi he addressed his assembled troops. Reminding them that they were at last near the end of their hardships and dangers, he asked them to be ready to leave behind in Italy their servants and baggage, and to embark alone without these encumbrances, so as to allow of a greater number of soldiers being taken on board; meanwhile to look forward to victory and his own generosity for supplying them with all their needs. His men answered with a cheer that he could order what he thought best, and that they would gladly obey whatever those orders might be. He accordingly set sail on the fourth of January,[8] with a fleet conveying, as already mentioned, seven legions of infantry. The following day he made the land hard by the Ceraunian mountains, and, finding an anchorage of calm water clear of the rocks and other dangerous spots, and carefully avoiding all harbors because these were suspected

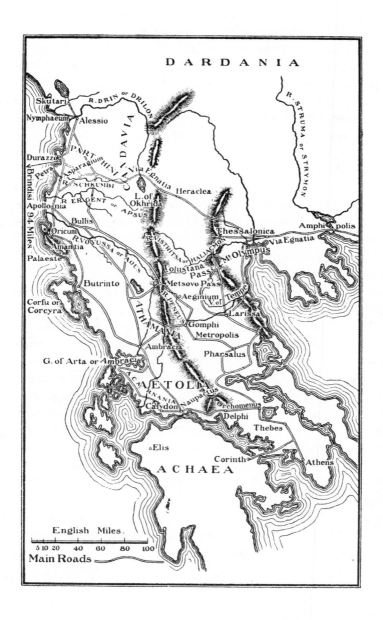

DARDANIA

Skutari
Nymphaeum
Alessio
R. DRIN or DRILON
DAVIA
R. STRUMA or STRYMON
Durazzo
Brindisi
Petra
Asparagium
PARTHINI
Via Egnatia
R. SCHKUMBI
Heraclea
R. ERGENT or APSUS
L. of Okhrida
Apollonia
Bullis
Oricum
Amantia
R.VOJUSSA or AOUS
R. MISTRITSA or HALIACMON
Thessalonica
Amphipolis
Palaeste
Via Egnatia
Mt. Olympus
Volustana Pass
Metsovo Pass
R. PENEUS
V. of Tempe
Butrinto
Corfu or Corcyra
ATHAMANIA
Aeginium
Larissa
Gomphi
Metropolis
Ambracia
Pharsalus
G. of Arta or Ambracia
ACARNANIA
AETOLIA
Calydon
Naupactus
Orchomenus
Delphi
Thebes
Elis
Corinth
Athens
ACHAEA

English Miles.
5 10 20   40   60   80   100
Main Roads

of being held by the enemy, disembarked his troops at a point called Palaeste, without the loss of a single transport.

At the time there was lying at Oricum[9] a detached squadron of eighteen ships of the Asiatic fleet under the command of Lucretius Vespillo and Minucius Rufus, acting under instructions from their admiral, Decimus Laelius; whilst further to the south lay Marcus Bibulus with 110 sail at Corfu (*Corcyra*). Of these two forces, however, the first-named had not the requisite self-confidence to leave the shelter of port, though Caesar's naval escort to his transports numbered no more than twelve ships of war, of which only four were decked; and Bibulus was caught with his vessels unprepared for action and his crews scattered on shore. As a consequence he came up too late, since Caesar was already sighted off the mainland before even the faintest rumor of his crossing had time to reach the neighborhood.

With the disembarkation completed, the transports were sent back that night to Brindisi to bring over the rest of the legions with the cavalry. This duty had been entrusted to Fufius Calenus, a general officer, in order to ensure promptitude in the work of transporting the legions. The ships unfortunately got off somewhat late, and, missing the advantage of the night breeze, encountered a serious disaster on their return journey. For Bibulus, informed at Corfu of Caesar's arrival, and hoping to succeed in falling in with at least a section of the laden troopships, fell in with the returning empties instead. Thirty of these or thereabouts he managed to secure, and, venting upon them the rage which his carelessness and consequent keen disappointment had excited, he burnt the entire lot, leaving the crews and masters to perish in the flames; his idea being that their comrades would be frightened from returning by the enormity of the punishment inflicted. This exploit accomplished, he proceeded to distribute his fleets in effective occupation of every roadstead and section of coast from the island of Sasino (*Sasonae*) in the south to Veglia (*Curicta*) in the north, his ships patrolling far and wide. Scouting squadrons were placed with greater care than hitherto, and, though it was the depth of winter, he yet persisted in keeping the sea with his blockading flotilla, resolved to shirk neither difficulty nor duty, even with no hope of relief in his arduous task, if only he could come to grips with Caesar.[10]

Following the withdrawal of the Liburnian fleet from Illyrian waters, the admiral, Marcus Octavius, with the division under his command, put in at Salonae.[11] There he stirred up Dalmatians and other native tribes, and succeeded in alienating the island of Lissa from its adherence to Caesar; but on attempting the same project with the Roman settlement at Salonae, he found that neither promises nor threats of reprisals could shake their allegiance, and therefore determined to carry the town by assault. Now this town has strong natural fortifications both from its general geographical position and from its commanding site on the crest of a hill. Notwithstanding, the Roman burghers at once took the further step of strengthening the defenses by a series of wooden towers along the walls; and, on finding that their slender numbers offered but a weak resistance to the attack, and that they were seriously incapacitated by repeated wounds, they had recourse to the desperate expedient of liberating all their able-bodied slaves, and even cut the hair from off all their women-folk in order to manufacture ropes necessary to the working of artillery.[12] When the news of their determination reached Octavius, he surrounded the city with five separate camps, and went on to press the garrison simultaneously by blockade and a series of concerted assaults. On their side the defenders were ready to continue the defense at any and every cost, but they suffered most severely from shortness of supplies. Agents were therefore dispatched to Caesar to petition his help in this one particular; every other kind of distress they continued to support unaided as best they could.

After the lapse of a considerable interval of time, it was noticed by the garrison that the long protraction of the siege had induced a certain carelessness among the troops of Octavius. They accordingly seized an opportunity whilst the besiegers were absent from their stations for the midday siesta; and, after posting women and children along the city wall so that no detail of the daily routine should be missed by the enemy, they formed a sortie-party from themselves and their recently liberated slaves, and dashed out upon the nearest of the Octavian camps. This they quickly stormed; and, following it up without a break by successive attacks on the second, third, fourth, and remaining camps in turn, they drove the Pompeians with great slaughter out of the whole series, and forced the remainder under Octavius to take shelter on board the fleet. This affair ended the siege; for, the winter now approaching, Octavius, after the heavy losses incurred, relinquished all hope of a successful assault on the town, and sailed away to rejoin Pompeius at Durazzo.

It has already been recorded how Lucius Vibullius Rufus, a sectional commander of Pompeius, had twice fallen into the hands of Caesar, and twice been released by him, viz. once at Pentima and a second time in Spain. The obligations thus conferred had induced Caesar to consider him an appropriate agent for sending to Pompeius with fresh proposals of peace, especially as he was understood to possess distinct influence with his chief. The general purport of these instructions was as follows.

Common prudence dictated that each party should now set a limit to its present attitude of uncompromising opposition, and, by agreeing to a cessation of hostilities, tempt Fortune no longer. They had both experienced defeats on a sufficiently serious scale to serve as a wholesome lesson for dreading further disasters. Whilst his opponent had been driven from Italy, and had lost Sicily, Sardinia, both Spanish provinces, and no less than 130 battalions of Roman troops, either in Italy itself or in Spain; he, on the other hand, had to mourn the death of Curio, the destruction of the army of Africa, and the surrender of Antonius and the force under him at Veglia. Should they not then cease to inflict these blows on themselves and their country, particularly when their own reverses had now abundantly shown them what a powerful factor is Fortune in war? The present moment offered a unique opportunity of treating for peace, at a time when each side still felt complete confidence in its own ultimate success, and whilst honors as yet seemed easy. If, however, Fortune, were now to give either belligerent even a trivial advantage, all terms would alike be rejected by what would then regard itself as the winning side, and equal stakes would no longer content the claimant who believed all to be in his grasp. The actual conditions of peace, whose settlements had hitherto been impossible, should be looked for at Rome, at the hands of the Senate and sovereign people: meanwhile it ought to be a sufficient guarantee to both their country and themselves, if each were at once to take an oath before his assembled troops to disband his army within three days after that event. By breaking up their organized forces and the auxiliary bodies on which they now relied, they would have no course left them but to abide by the decision of the Senate and people.

Such were the proposals now forwarded by Caesar, and, in order to facilitate their acceptance by Pompeius, he made the further concession that he was ready to disband the whole of his field army and all garrisons in the towns.[13]

Now Vibullius had landed at Corfu; but, thinking it of at least equal importance that Pompeius should be informed of Caesar's sudden arrival on the coast, so as to take his counter-measures before the subject of the peace proposals was broached, he immediately posted off to meet him; and, traveling night and day, with relays of fresh cattle at every town to ensure greater speed, brought the intelligence that Caesar had landed. Pompeius was at this time in Candavia,[14] on his way to his army's winter quarters[14] in Apollonia and Durazzo; but Vibullius' news was so alarming that he at once began to quicken his march towards Apollonia, with the object of preventing his rival's occupation of the coast towns. Caesar, however, had only waited till his troops were all disembarked before marching upon Oricum. On his appearance before that town, the Pompeian governor of the place, Lucius Torquatus, endeavored to make a show of resistance by means of his garrison of Parthini, and orders were given to close the gates. But his Greek troops, when commanded to man the walls and take up arms, flatly refused to act in opposition to a duly elected representative of the Roman Government; and when their refusal was accompanied by an independent attempt on the part of the townspeople to admit

Caesar, Torquatus gave up the situation as hopeless, and, directing the gates to be opened, surrendered himself and the town to Caesar, by whom he was treated with all the honors of war.

Halting merely to take over the surrendered town, Caesar at once started for Apollonia. Upon the news of his advance reaching the governor, Lucius Staberius, that officer proceeded to move a supply of water into the citadel of the town and to throw up fortifications for its defense; at the same time demanding hostages from the townsfolk for their good behavior. But not only did these decline to give any such guarantees, but they openly declared they would never shut their gates in a consul's face, or set up their own private judgment against the unanimous verdict of Italy and the Roman world. Staberius, therefore, recognizing the firm attitude of the citizens, had no choice left him but a secret flight from the town; whereupon the inhabitants dispatched an embassy to Caesar and threw open their city to his approach. Their example was followed by the people of Bullis and Amantia and other neighboring townships, and by practically the whole of Epirus, envoys arriving from all quarters to assure him of their readiness to submit to his orders.

Meanwhile the result of these opening operations at Oricum and Apollonia made Pompeius extremely anxious for the safety of his base at Durazzo (*Dyrrachium*), and he was now marching night and day upon that city. Simultaneously the rumor spread that Caesar was close on his heels; a report that created such violent panic in Pompeius' army after his frantic haste in turning night into day and in marching his men without a halt, that virtually all the troops hailing from Epirus and its immediate neighborhood deserted their ranks, many of them actually flinging away their arms, and the whole march degenerating into something like a rout. This disgraceful panic was not even stayed with their safe arrival before Durazzo; and accordingly, when the usual order had been given to mark out the camp boundaries, Labienus, in order to check the demoralization, stepped forward and solemnly swore that he would never desert Pompeius, but would share with him any and every lot that fortune might decree. This same oath was taken by all the other generals present, followed by the regimental officers and centurions; after which the whole of the rank and file swore to observe the same. As for Caesar, on finding his march upon Durazzo anticipated, he gave up the chase, and pitched his camp near the river Ergent (*Apsus*), within the territories of Apollonia—a position which enabled him to protect by a ring of fortified outposts the townships which had recently served him so loyally. Here he determined to await the arrival of the rest of his legions from Italy, and to go under canvas[16] for winter. The same resolution was also taken by Pompeius, who now entrenched himself on the opposite or northern bank of the Ergent, and proceeded to concentrate within his new lines the whole of his regular and auxiliary forces.

Meanwhile Calenus, in execution of his orders received from Caesar, had embarked the legions and cavalry at Brindisi as far as his supply of transports allowed, and, setting sail, had got some little distance from port, when he was met by a dispatch-boat from Caesar with intelligence that the whole of the opposite harbors and shores were effectually held by the enemy's fleets. Upon this information, he at once put back towards harbor, and signalled the recall to his remaining convoy. A single ship, however, kept on her course, and refused to acknowledge the admiral's signal, since she had no troops on board, but was sailing under private orders. She was carried down the Illyrian coast to Oricum, and there captured by Bibulus; who, exacting the full penalty alike from slaves and free, and even beardless boys, massacred every living soul on board.

On so short a space of time, and on so mere a chance, hung the safety of the whole army.

It will have been noticed from the above that Bibulus with his fleet was now at Oricum, where a singular military position had developed itself. On his side, his blockading squadrons effectually deprived Caesar of all control both of the sea and its harbors; whilst his own force was no less completely debarred from every inch of ground along the same territories: for, the whole of the foreshore being safely held by Caesar's pickets and patrols, the Pompeians had no means either of watering their ships and supplying them with fuel, or of mooring them to the beach. So impossible, indeed, grew the situation, and so hard pressed were they for the barest necessaries of life, that they were forced to employ cargo-boats to bring up from Corfu, not merely the ordinary requirements for victualling a fleet, but even their very firewood and drinking-water. To aggravate their sufferings, there came a period of contrary winds, during which they were actually driven to collect the night dew off the skins which served as awnings to their ships. Yet these sufferings were borne with cheerful resignation, nor was there any thought of withdrawing their watch upon the harbors or of leaving the coast uncovered.

It was during the critical state of their supplies as just described, and after Libo had rejoined Bibulus at Oricum with the division under his command, that these two officers addressed a petition in common from the decks of their flagships to Manius Acilius and Statius Murcus, the Caesarian military authorities in that region—the former in charge of the town fortifications, the latter of the shore-defenses—to the effect that, if their request could be complied with, they desired an audience with Caesar on a matter of most vital import.

A few remarks were added by way of confirmation of their statement, and to give the impression that the subject of a settlement was to be brought forward; and meanwhile, until the interview could be arranged, they requested an armistice, which was accordingly granted them by the Caesarian officers. For not only did the message conveyed appear to them of considerable moment, but they well knew how sincerely anxious Caesar was for an opening of this nature, whilst what weighed with them further was the belief that the overtures lately initiated by Vibullius had apparently met with some measure of success.

At the particular time Caesar happened to be absent from Oricum, having lately left with a single legion to receive the surrender of the more distant townships, and also to improve his commissariat department, which was supplying him but indifferently. He was now at Butrinto (*Buthrotum*), a coast town just opposite to Corfu; but, upon receiving dispatches from Acilius and Murcus informing him of the demands put forward by Libo and Bibulus, he left the legion behind and at once returned to Oricum. There, on his arrival, he invited the two Pompeian chiefs to a conference. Only Libo made his appearance, excusing the absence of Bibulus, which, doubtless, was prompted by his excessively hot temper, and by the fact that, in addition to political differences, he had long nursed a private quarrel with Caesar, originating in the years of their common aedileship and praetorship.[17] "For this reason," said Libo, "his colleague had now avoided meeting his opponent, in order that his own temper might not prove an obstacle to the success of proceedings which promised so well for the future."

With this introduction, he proceeded to assure Caesar that the most earnest desire of Pompeius was, and had always been, for a peaceful settlement and cessation from hostilities; but that they could not give practical effect to their commander's wishes, because the whole conduct of the campaign and of all other questions alike had been made over to him absolutely by a decree of their council of war. If, however, Caesar would acquaint them with the nature of his demands, they would forward these to Pompeius, who would then conduct the rest of the negotiations directly with him, receiving the while every support from themselves. In the interval, until an answer could be returned from Pompeius, they asked for the armistice to hold good, and no hostile measure to be taken by either belligerent. This included all that was pertinent in his proposals, though certain remarks were added about his own cause and about the armed forces under his command; remarks which Caesar both ignored at the time, as not necessitating an answer, and which today we see no sufficient reason for putting upon record.

His own definite demands were then formulated as follows:

He must either be allowed to send representatives to Pompeius without let or hindrance, and with a safe-conduct guaranteed by Libo and his colleagues, or else the latter could themselves take his officers on board and be responsible for conveying them to Pompeius. As for the question of armistice, they must look to the strategical position of the two combatants, which was so peculiarly balanced that, whilst they with their fleet blocked his ships and reinforcements, he, on the other hand, cut them off from their watering and from all communication with the shore. If they wanted this privation relaxed, they must relax their watch on the sea: if, on the contrary, that was maintained, he would retain his hold on the land. However, there was no reason why peace negotiations should not equally well be conducted under the *status quo,* nor did the one state of things constitute any obstacle to the other.

In answer to this, Libo replied that he could neither undertake to receive Caesar's delegates on board, nor could he guarantee their safe-conduct; he could only refer the whole matter for decision to Pompeius. The one point that he steadily urged was the truce, and for that he contended with extraordinary passion. Caesar, therefore, realizing that the whole proceedings had simply been instituted with the sole object of escaping their present dangerous situation and shortness of supplies, and that Libo was in a position to offer no genuine prospect or proposal for peace, broke off the discussion, and returned to the task of perfecting his plans for the war.

As for Libo's colleague Bibulus, his long exclusion from the shore was presently complicated by serious sickness, the result of exposure to cold and constant work; and, suitable treatment being impossible, whilst he steadily refused to quit the post of duty, his constitution proved unequal to withstanding the disease. Upon his death, the supreme naval command was not again vested in any single authority; but the various divisional fleets acted independently of each other, according to the caprice of their respective admirals.

With respect to Vibullius and his mission, as soon as the tumult excited by Caesar's sudden arrival had abated, and the first opportunity occurred after his own return to the coast, he had secured an interview with Pompeius. To this interview there were also admitted Libo, Lucius Lucceius, and Theophanes, the three confidential advisers with whom Pompeius habitually conferred on high matters of state; and Vibullius then proceeded to unfold the instructions received from Caesar. He had barely commenced speaking when Pompeius cut him short with an order to say no more. "What value," he exclaimed, "will life or country possess for me, when I shall be thought to retain them merely on the sufferance of Caesar? an opinion that nothing will get rid of, if people come to regard me as fetched back to Italy, after having freely departed from it."

This incident came to Caesar's knowledge at the close of the war, from those who were present at the speech; yet, in spite of this latest failure, he still continued his efforts to open up through other channels verbal negotiations for peace.

The method next tried was as follows.

The two opposing camps were separated solely by the river Ergent (*Apus*), and, as a consequence, frequent communications passed to and fro between the rival troops; the speakers mutually agreeing that no hostile shot should be fired across the stream during these meetings. Caesar accordingly commissioned Publius Vatinius, a staff officer, to go down to the very edge of the river bank, with powers to discuss the basis of a settlement, and to ask repeatedly in tones plainly audible whether citizens were not permitted to send a pair of peace envoys to fellow citizens—a concession hitherto allowed even to runaway slaves among the Pyrenean passes, and to defeated pirates[18]—above all when their sole object was the prevention of an armed struggle between Romans and Romans. In execution of this charge Vatinius spoke at considerable length, and with the earnestness of appeal rightly demanded where the vital interests both of himself and of the civilized world were at stake, and his words were listened to in silence by the soldiers of either army. An answer was returned from the side of the Pompeians that Aulus Varro pledged himself to appear at a conference on the following day, and, further, to take measures for ensuring our envoys both a safe-conduct and absolute freedom of speech. A time was accordingly fixed for this meeting; and on the morrow, at the appointed hour, large numbers assembled from both sides, in eager anticipation of the event, and with every man's thoughts seemingly intent on peace. Out of this throng there then stepped Titus Labienus, who in quiet conversational tones began a speech on the subject of peace, and to enter on a debate with Vatinius. In the midst of their discussion, they were suddenly interrupted by a shower of spears flung from every quarter; and, although Vatinius managed to escape by the intervention of his soldiers' shields, several others were wounded, including Cornelius Balbus, Marcus Plotius, and Lucius Tiburtius, as well as some centurions and privates. Thereupon Labienus exclaimed, "It is nonsense, you see, to talk of a settlement: until we have Caesar's head, there can be no peace between us."

CHAPTER TWO

A BACKWATER
OF THE REVOLUTION

CONTEMPORARY WITH THESE EVENTS ABROAD THERE HAD BEEN certain serious trouble in the capital at home, where Marcus Caelius Rufus, one of the praetors for the year, had taken on himself to champion the cause of the debtor classes. After entering upon his official duties, he had established his magisterial dais alongside the judicial chair of his colleague the city praetor, Caius Trebonius, and there proceeded to promise his official support to any who chose to appeal on the valuation of their property and the enforced payments of liabilities that were now being carried out by the verdict of individual arbitrators, in accordance with the measure adopted by Caesar during his late stay in Rome. So essentially fair, however, was this measure in itself, and so wise a toleration did Trebonius exhibit in executing its terms, from conviction that the times called for a considerate and temperate dispensation of justice, that no parties were forthcoming to initiate the process of appeal. The truth is that, whilst very ordinary courage is required to plead poverty and declaim against one's own personal troubles or those of the times, and to lay before the court the hardships attending an enforced sale; to keep entire possession of property, admittedly due to another, argues the very height of assurance, not to say effrontery. Consequently no one could be found to put forward so extravagant a demand; and Caelius was left to prove himself more intractable than even the parties for whom he was professedly acting. For, once started on his career, he had now to avoid the fiasco of having undertaken a discreditable piece of business with nothing to show for it: he therefore brought forward a measure by which all debts were to be discharged without accumulation of interest that day six years.

This proposal naturally met with opposition from the consul Servilius and the rest of the Government; and Caelius, baulked of his expectations, determined to make a bid for the support of the populace. Withdrawing his earlier law, he now substituted two others in its place; in the first of which he made a present of a year's rent to every tenant of an inhabited house, and in the second announced a general cancelling of debts: and further he instigated the mob to a brutal attack against Caius Trebonius, who was hustled off his magisterial platform, whilst several others were wounded. These proceedings were reported by Servilius to the Senate, and the Chamber resolved that Caelius had deserved suspension from public functions. Acting on this decree, the consul then forbade him the House, and when he subsequently endeavored to address the assembled people outside, ordered his forcible removal from the rostra.[1] This last open disgrace stung him to resentment; and, giving out in public that he was leaving Rome to go off to Caesar, he secretly sent agents to Milo, then under sentence of exile upon the charge of murdering Clodius, and invited him into Italy. Milo he considered a useful tool for his purpose, because the lavish public games formerly exhibited by him in the city had still left him with a remnant of his old gladiatorial gang. A junction was effected between the two, and Milo was then sent on in advance to raise the herdsmen in the regions round Thurii. Caelius himself came down to Casilinum; only, however, to hear that all his regimental colors[2] and stacks of arms had been seized at Capua, and that the band of hired bravoes, which was to contrive the treacherous surrender of Naples (*Neapolis*), had been discovered in that city. The plot now stood revealed, and Capua in consequence shut its gates against him; even personal danger was to be feared, since the district had taken up arms and was now inclined to treat him as a common outlaw. He therefore broke off his present design, and retired from his advance in these regions.

In the meantime Milo was distributing a proclamation among the Italian municipalities, to the effect that he was acting under the express orders of Pompeius, received in the form of instructions from Vibullius; and on the strength of this artifice was endeavoring to win the support of any whom he had reason to suspect of being in money difficulties. These last failing to respond, he proceeded to break open some private slave compounds, and then to lay siege to the town of Cosa, situated in the territories of Thurii. A legion was at once dispatched to its relief by Quintus Pedius, one of the praetors, and Milo was subsequently killed by a stone that struck him from the city wall. As for Caelius, maintaining his assertion that he was on his way to Caesar, he got as far as Thurii. There he tried to tamper with certain of the city authorities; but on offering a bribe to the Caesarian cavalry, composed of Gallic and Spanish horse, who had been sent down to garrison the place, he met with his death at their hands. In this way what threatened to develop into a serious movement, and, owing to the preoccupation of the Government with the crisis abroad, was giving rise to serious anxiety in Italy, came to an easy and a speedy termination.

CHAPTER THREE

THE LINES OF DYRRACHIUM

To RESUME THE NARRATIVE OF THE CAMPAIGN. IT WAS ABOUT THIS time that a naval demonstration against Italy was organized under Libo, who, with the fleet of fifty ships of the line under his immediate command, set sail from Oricum and crossed to Brindisi, where he seized as his base the island commanding the entrance to that harbor.[1] This plan he adopted because he considered it sounder strategy to concentrate his attention upon a single point where our forces must inevitably pass out to sea, than to maintain a blockade of all the adjacent shores and harbors. His sudden arrival on the coast enabled him to pick up a few stray merchantmen: these he all promptly burned, excepting one with a cargo of corn which was brought back by its captors as a prize. Altogether he created no little panic amongst our people; and this was further increased by a successful night attack, in which a landing-party of legionaries and archers dislodged one of our mounted pickets. His strong position, indeed, gained him such marked advantages, that, in a dispatch to Pompeius, he assured his commanding officer that, if he liked, he might give orders for the rest of the fleet to go into dock and refit, since his own squadron would effectually block up the reinforcements destined for Caesar.

Fortunately at this moment Antonius was at Brindisi. Placing implicit reliance on the high quality of his troops, this officer selected some sixty ships' cutters from his larger transports, which he then proceeded to cover with a superstructure of fascines and mantlets.

On board of these a picked body of legionaries was next embarked, and the boats were then stationed in detachments at various points along the shore. This done, orders were given for two three-deckers,[2] lately built under his supervision at Brindisi, to row out to the mouth of the harbor under the pretence of exercising the crews. Noticing the boldness with which they came on, Libo conceived the hope of cutting off their retreat, and detached five of his four-deckers[3] against them. These had approached to within a short distance of our vessels, when our crews, veterans though supposed to be, were suddenly seen to go about and to be running for the shelter of port; on which the Pompeians, with more enthusiasm than caution, at once commenced to pursue. Suddenly, on the given signal, out shot from every quarter the Antonian launches, racing up to the enemy. Singling out one of the four-deckers, they captured her at the first burst with all her navigating[4] and fighting crews, whilst her consorts sought safety in a disgraceful flight.

This disaster was soon afterwards followed by another. Antonius having stationed a chain of mounted patrols along the foreshore, the enemy found himself deprived of all access to water; so that Libo, feeling his position to be as untenable as it was undignified, was forced to evacuate Brindisi, and to relinquish the blockade of our reinforcements waiting there.

Many months had now elapsed, and winter was well past its climax, whilst yet there was no sign of the transports with the legions crossing from Brindisi to Caesar. Moreover, it appeared to Caesar that several opportunities for making the passage had been neglected, since the wind had certainly blown from the quarter which, in his judgment, was essential for putting to sea. What made the delay more serious was that, the further the season advanced, the greater grew the energy displayed by the enemy's naval commanders in their watch upon the coast, and the higher rose their hopes of successfully preventing our crossing. Frequent dispatches also came down from Pompeius, conveying severe reprimands on their failure to stop Caesar in his first voyage, and urgent exhortations to see that the rest of his armament was not similarly allowed to cross the straits; and they were now daily reckoning on the change of season when lighter winds would increase the difficulties of transporting an army. All these considerations induced Caesar to dispatch a somewhat peremptory order to his agents at Brindisi,[5] bidding them at the first fair wind not to lose a chance of sailing, if once they could shape such a course as to hit the opposite coast within the boundaries of Apollonia and there run their vessels ashore. These regions, it should be explained, were the freest from the blockading squadrons, owing to the enemy's nervousness about venturing far from his ports.

His officers responded with intrepid courage. Whilst Marcus Antonius and Fufius Calenus jointly directed the embarkation, the men themselves eagerly seconded their efforts in their readiness to brave all risks for ensuring the safety of Caesar; and having secured a southerly wind they weighed anchor, and the next day were swept up the coast past Apollonia and Durazzo. As soon as they were sighted from the mainland, Caius Coponius, the admiral commanding the Rhodian fleet at Durazzo, at once rowed his ships out of harbor, and, the breeze slackening, got close up with our transports; but at that moment the southerly gale once more freshened, and by so doing saved our vessels from certain capture. This, however, was not enough to turn Coponius from his purpose; and, trusting the unflagging efforts of his crews to be more than a match for the pace of the gale, he kept up the chase even after his opponents had been blown past Durazzo by the great force of the wind. On the other hand, our ships, though fully profiting by their stroke of goodluck, still dreaded an attack from the armed fleet, if once the wind should moderate. Gaining the harbor therefore called Nymphaeum, three miles beyond Alessio (*Lissus*), they steered their ships into it; and though it is sheltered from a southwesterly gale and exposed to a southerly, they yet felt they had less to fear from the hurricane than from the enemy's pursuing squadron. They were, however, no sooner inside, than the wind, which for two days had blown steadily from the south, with a good fortune wellnigh incredible, veered to the southwest.

Sudden indeed was the turning of the tables now witnessed. Those who a moment before had feared for their very lives were now within the shelter of an absolutely safe harbor: those on the other hand, who had just threatened our vessels with destruction, had now to look to their own. So completely were the conditions reversed, that, whilst to our men the fresh gale proved a direct preservation, it caught the Rhodian men-of-war with such violence that everyone of their decked ships, sixteen in all, were driven ashore and went to pieces on the rocks. Of the large numbers forming their navigating and fighting crews, part were dashed upon the cliffs and killed, others were rescued by our troops; these last being all spared by Caesar and given a free passage home.

Two of our transports unfortunately were a little late in completing their voyage, and accordingly were overtaken by night. Not knowing at what point the rest of the convoy had made the coast, they lay off at anchor opposite Alessio (*Lissus*). Thereupon the Pompeian commandant of the place, Otacilius Crassus, put out with a large number of ships' boats and other small craft, and commenced preparations for boarding; in the meanwhile discussing terms of surrender and guaranteeing fair treatment to the prisoners. (One of the ships, it should be mentioned, had on board 220 recruits from a newly raised legion, the other a trifle under two hundred from a corps of veterans.)

Then occurred a signal illustration of the self-defense that lies in undaunted courage. The recruits, frightened by the swarm of boats, and prostrated with seasickness and the effects of their voyage, accepted the sworn word of the enemy not to injure them, and surrendered to Otacilius. They were at once marched off to the governor; and there, in his presence, in defiance of his solemn oath, were brutally massacred to a man. On the other hand, the veteran contingent, though equally shaken by their cramped position in the ship's hold, which had been rendered still worse by the storm, braced themselves to maintain unsullied the lofty reputation of their corps; and by haggling over terms, and pretending to be always on the point of surrender, succeeded in wearing away the first part of the night. They then compelled their captain to run his ship ashore, and, finding there a defensible position, passed the rest of the night upon it. At dawn a body of cavalry, some four hundred strong, forming the regular patrol of that section of the coast, was dispatched against them by Otacilius, to be shortly afterwards followed by a force of heavy-armed infantry from the town garrison; but against both alike they made good their defense, and after inflicting several casualties upon the enemy, without any loss whatever to themselves, successfully effected a retirement upon their head quarters.

Immediately after this the Roman settlement in Alessio (*Lissus*), which at this time was responsible for the government of the city, Caesar having on a previous occasion attached it to their jurisdiction, and at the same time provided for its fortification, sent out a warm welcome to Antony, putting everything they possessed at the disposal of his army. Thereupon Otacilius, becoming apprehensive for his own position, hastily withdrew his garrison from the town, and rejoined Pompeius.

Meanwhile Antonius, after completing the disembarkation of his reinforcements, amounting in all to three veteran and one conscript legion with nine hundred mounted troops, sent back the majority of his transports to Italy, with orders to convey across the remaining infantry and cavalry; leaving, however, at Alessio a batch of large sailing punts—a species of Gallic craft—in order that, should Pompeius again throw his army across into Italy under the belief that it was now denuded of troops (a plan with which rumor commonly credited him), Caesar should at least retain some means of pursuit. He then sent off express messengers to his commander-in-chief, informing him both of the place of his landing and of the strength of the forces accompanying him.

Now it so happened that information on these two points reached Caesar and Pompeius almost simultaneously. They had both witnessed the transports driving with the storm past Apollonia and Durazzo, and had themselves at once started overland on their track; in ignorance, however, for the first few days, of the particular point at which the ships had made the coast. The receipt of this further intelligence caused the adoption by the rival commanders of two mutually exclusive plans; Caesar aiming at a junction with Antonius at the earliest possible moment, Pompeius endeavoring to intercept the new arrivals on their march southward, with a chance perhaps also of surprising them by ambush. Accordingly each broke up his permanent quarters along the Ergent (*Apsus*) within twenty-four hours of the other, but whereas Pompeius secretly set his army in motion during the night, Caesar marched out in the light of open day. The latter had the longer route before him, as a considerable detour was involved by the necessity of first marching up-stream before a crossing could be effected; in the meantime Pompeius could get off with a clear road without any river to ford, and push on to meet Antony by a series of forced marches. With the intelligence that his opponent was now close at hand, he selected a suitable site for encamping, and there settled down to await his arrival; keeping all arms strictly within his lines, and as a further precaution allowing no fires to be lighted. These movements were promptly reported to Antonius by the local Greek population; so that Antony, after dispatching runners to advise Caesar of the same, remained that day quietly in camp; and on the next Caesar marched in with his men. The news of their junction made Pompeius anxious lest he should find himself surrounded by the two allied armies; he therefore fell back from the neighborhood and marched in force to Asparagium, a town belonging to Durazzo, where on some strong ground a new camp was fortified.

Whilst the war had thus been in progress some considerable time, Scipio had all along been busy in the East. After first suffering several defeats in the region of Mount Amanus, on the strength of which he had acclaimed himself Commander,[6] he had followed up these exploits by levying large contributions of money upon the townships and petty sovereigns of his province of Syria. The arrears of taxes, owing for the last two years, had been squeezed out of the contractors,[7] who had been compelled to make a further advance on mortgage of the estimates for the ensuing year; at the same time a cavalry conscription had been ordered over the entire province. As soon as this force was ready he turned his back upon his immediate enemy, the Parthians—an enemy who had in the last few years caused the death of Marcus Crassus, the well-known commander, and had since kept Marcus Bibulus shut up within siege lines—and withdrew from Syria its garrison of legions and mounted troops. Such a step produced the gravest anxiety and apprehensions of a Parthian war throughout the province, apprehensions which were soon echoed by not infrequent murmurs among the troops, who made it known that if their march was to be directed against a national enemy they would cheerfully follow, but that against a fellow citizen and the first magistrate of the state they would never draw a sword.

At these symptoms of possible trouble, Scipio hit upon the device of quartering his soldiers upon Bergama (*Pergamum*) and the other rich cities of Asia Minor; and here he not only indulged them with the most extravagant largesses, but, further to whet their appetite for the campaign, handed them over the townships to plunder.

While the troops were thus engaged, the unhappy provincials had everywhere to find the money required to meet the grinding exactions of the authorities. Many novel heads of taxation were devised at the bidding of official cupidity. A poll-tax was levied on every head of the population, whether slave or free; taxes on house pillars, taxes on doors, a money composition for the army's corn supply, for troops, accoutrements, ships' crews, ordnance, and transport; in short, they had only to find a sufficiently plausible title, and it was at once pronounced an adequate instrument for the raising of fresh funds. Commandants possessed of full military powers were quartered, not merely in the large cities, but one might almost say in every individual hamlet and hill fortress of the province; and those who distinguished themselves in the work of plunder by any remarkable cruelty or rapacity were rewarded by a reputation for exceptional ability and patriotism. Asia Minor was completely overrun with the holders of military authority and their dreaded attendants;[8] it was crammed with officials and tax-gatherers. These men, in addition to the legal sum demanded, were not above doing a bit of business on their own account; the excuse constantly urged was that, as they had been driven from home and country, they were now in need of the common necessaries of life; and by this plea they endeavored to cloak under a specious title of respectability their most disreputable proceedings. A further calamity for the provincials was the exorbitant rise in interest, a not unusual phenomenon in time of war, where a whole community is called upon to furnish ready money; and, in the hardships thus entailed, any postponement by the creditors of the day of settlement was magnified into a free gift to the unfortunate debtors. In this way the capital debt of the province more than doubled itself during these two years. Yet it is not to be supposed that the Roman citizens settled in the province were therefore allowed to go exempt. Fixed sums were apportioned for each administrative area, for each individual township; and the authors of these forced contributions invariably represented them as loans negotiated on the authority of the Senate's decree. Finally, the farmers of the imperial revenues were compelled, as they had previously been in Syria, to advance the proceeds of the tribute for the ensuing year.

In addition to all these sources of income, Scipio did not scruple to order the removal from the great temple of Diana at Ephesus of the treasures accumulated there from immemorial antiquity. On the day appointed for this sacrilege an entrance into the sacred building had already been effected by himself and a party of the senatorial order, who had been expressly summoned to witness the act, when dispatches from Pompeius were put into his hand, bearing the information that Caesar had crossed the water with a part of his legions, and containing urgent instructions to hasten the advance of his army towards a junction with his chief, to which every other interest was to be subordinated. On receipt of this intelligence he at once dismissed the invited senators and commenced preparations for his march into Macedonia, upon which he started a few days later; his recall thus proving the salvation of the Ephesian treasures.

We must now retrace the interrupted narrative of Caesar's own movements. The successful junction with the army of Antony enabled him, he thought, to withdraw the single legion at Oricum, previously stationed there for the defense of that part of the coast, and so, by extending the area of his operations, to test the feeling of the neighboring provinces. Envoys had already reached him from Thessaly and Livadia (*Aetolia*), charged with the duty of conveying the assurance that the towns of these regions only required the presence of a garrison in order to put themselves completely at his disposal. Three distinct expeditions were accordingly now taken in hand. In the first place, Lucius Cassius Longinus was sent into Thessaly at the head of a single legion of conscripts (the Twenty-seventh) and two hundred mounted men: secondly, Caius Calvisius Sabinus was commissioned to invade Livadia with five battalions of infantry and a troop of horse; both these officers receiving most earnest instructions to organize in those immediately outlying districts a regular supply of corn for the main army: whilst lastly, Cnaeus Domitius Calvinus had orders to march into Macedonia with two legions—the Eleventh and Twelfth— and a cavalry force of six hundred sabres. The principal reason for this third enterprise was the presence in camp of the chieftain Menedemus, the most powerful ruler in what is known as "Independent" Macedonia, who had been dispatched to Caesar as special envoy from his subjects, and who was now promising the enthusiastic and unanimous devotion of his followers.

Of these three expeditions that under Calvisius, from the first day of its arrival in Livadia (*Aetolia*), received the warmest support from all parties: the enemy's garrisons in Kurtaga[9] and Lepanto (*Calydon* and *Naupactus*) were driven out, and complete possession gained of the country. Cassius also with his one legion successfully penetrated into Thessaly; but the existence here of two rival political factions produced considerable variety in the character of the reception accorded him by the several states. The leader of one of these factions was Hegesaretos, a chief of long-established power, devoted to the interests of Pompeius: opposed to him was Petraeus, a scion of one of their noblest families, who, together with his party, now brought to the cause of Caesar the strenuous support of their combined resources. Simultaneous with both these was the arrival in Macedonia of the third force under Domitius. Here ambassadors from the provincial centers were already gathering in considerable numbers to meet the Caesarian representative, when the movement was suddenly checked by the announcement of Scipio's near approach, heralded as it was on all sides by extravagant opinions concerning the powers of the new commander: it being common experience in all novelty for reputation to precede performance. The newcomer, making no halt anywhere in Macedonia, pushed on vigorously in the direction of Domitius, until he was now no more than twenty miles apart. He then suddenly turned south into Thessaly against Cassius Longinus, executing this flank movement with such startling rapidity that the news of his approach actually coincided with that of his arrival. Moreover, to make his march the quicker, he left behind at the river Vistritza (*Haliacmon*) (the boundary between Macedonia and Thessaly), a force of eight battalions under Marcus Favonius, as a guard to the baggage-trains of his legions, with orders to construct a fort upon that river.

Whilst thus engaged himself, it happened that the cavalry force of King Cotys, which was habitually hovering on the outskirts of Thessaly, swooped down upon the camp of Cassius: whereupon that commander, thoroughly alarmed by the news of Scipio's arrival on the scene, and mistaking the cavalry he saw for that of the Pompeian general, set his troops in motion for the western part of the mountain range that girdles the whole of Thessaly, and thence began a retirement in the direction of Arta (*Ambracia*). Scipio on his side was vigorously pressing the pursuit, when he was shortly overtaken by a dispatch from Favonius announcing the presence of Domitius with his two legions, and informing his commanding officer that unless reinforced he could not defend the fortified post where he had been stationed. The receipt of this dispatch caused Scipio to make a complete change both in his plans and in the direction of his march. Breaking off the pursuit of Cassius, he now hastened to the relief of Favonius; and by marching night and day without a halt, he succeeded in rejoining his lieutenant under such remarkably fortunate circumstances, that the rising dust of Domitius' army was already observed just as the leading vedettes of Scipio first came into sight. Thus Cassius was saved by the energetic conduct of Domitius, and Favonius by the rapidity of Scipio.

The last-named commander now rested two days inside his permanent fortifications on the river Vistritza, which separated him from Domitius on the northern bank: on the third day at dawn his army crossed by a ford and proceeded to erect a camp; on the fourth his line of battle was drawn up along the front of the new entrenchments. Once more Domitius was prompt to meet the challenge, and resolved to advance his legions and then and there to accept the issue of a pitched battle. Between the two rival camps, however, there intervened an open plain some six miles broad: this the Caesarians had first to cross, and then marshalled their line beneath the higher ground of Scipio, who still persisted in his determination not to come down from his entrenchments. The result was that in spite of the difficulties of restraining the eager Domitian infantry, no actual encounter as yet ensued; the chief obstacle being a small stream running under Scipio's camp, whose awkward banks presented considerable difficulties to our advance. Yet Scipio had seen enough of the high mettle of our troops and their eagerness to engage, to induce the suspicion that on the morrow he would either be forced to fight against his will, or else suffer a serious blow in reputation, if he still kept behind the shelter of his breastworks, especially after the high expectations formed of his intervention in the campaign. His first presumptuous advance thus ended somewhat ingloriously, and under cover of night, without even venturing to sound the usual signal for striking camp, he silently transferred his army across the river, and once more returned to his original quarters, where on some natural heights close by the stream a fresh camp was constructed. A few days of inaction then followed, at the close of which a surprise attack by ambush was planned against our forces by the Pompeian leader, who placed a body of cavalry at a spot where on previous days we had generally gone out for forage. Accordingly, on the next morning, when Quintus Varus, the cavalry commander in Domitius' army, paid his daily visit to the place, his troopers were suddenly set upon by the concealed horsemen. A stout resistance was nevertheless offered to the attack, and, quickly rallying on their respective troops, the united Caesarian cavalry delivered a counterattack upon their assailants. Some eighty saddles were emptied, and, after completing the rout of the remainder, the foraging party rode back to camp, having sustained in all but two casualties.

These initial operations raised some expectation in Domitius that Scipio might perhaps be enticed to a general engagement. Pretending, therefore, that shortness of supplies now compelled him to change his ground, he ordered the regular military signal to be sounded for striking camp, preparatory to marching a distance of three miles. There he found a site conveniently hidden from view, and on it proceeded to dispose the whole of his effective army, including the mounted troops. Scipio was equally ready to follow, and for this purpose advanced a reconnoitring force of cavalry to ascertain the precise route taken by his opponent. This force proceeding to its appointed task, its leading squadrons had already ridden into the ambush awaiting it, when the champing of our horses by rousing their suspicions caused them to commence retiring upon their supports: similarly the succeeding files, on noticing the hasty retreat of their comrades, drew themselves to the halt. The trap was now disclosed, and the Caesarians, perceiving the uselessness of waiting the arrival of the remaining squadrons, closed in on the two successfully caught, capturing along with them the cavalry leader Marcus Opimius. The rest of the two troops were either cut to pieces in the *mêlée* or captured and brought prisoners to Domitius.

Meanwhile, as already related, Caesar had recalled all the detachments lately holding the southern coastline, excepting three battalions left behind at Oricum to garrison that city. These troops he now further entrusted with the task of guarding his small fleet of warships originally brought over with the expedition from Italy. The officer selected for this twofold duty was Manius Acilius, who at once proceeded to move the vessels round into the inner harbor behind the town, and there to moor them against the shore. He next blocked the mouth of the harbor with a sunken merchantman, to which was attached a second and similar craft, and upon their decks erected a wooden military tower, forming a barrier immediately in the line of the fairway. This tower was given a full complement of legionaries, and the troops were then made responsible for its safe defense against any surprise by sea. Information of these dispositions duly reached the younger Cnaeus Pompeius, the admiral commanding the Egyptian squadron. He at once sailed for Oricum, and after first removing the sunken merchantman, by hauling on her with a series of tow-ropes, he proceeded to attack the second, or guard-ship of Acilius, by means of the concentrated fire of a number of his own vessels. These had been specially fitted with siege-towers, raised upon deck to a level that gave them the upper hand of their opponents: hence, by constantly bringing up fresh reserves to the relief of his exhausted crews, and endeavoring to divide the strength of the defense by pressing the attack against the city walls at all other points practicable, as well by escalade on land as by bombardment from the fleet at sea, the Pompeian admiral at length broke down the stubborn resistance of the Caesarian garrison. Compelled at last by sheer exhaustion and the torrent of spears to which they were exposed to quit their posts, they all succeeded in escaping by the boats, leaving the guard-ship to be afterwards captured as a prize by the enemy. At the moment of this success the Pompeians also established a footing in the rear of the defense, on the natural breakwater that in course of time had converted the town of Oricum into a peninsula. This advantage they utilized to mount upon rollers four of their two-deckers,[10] which they then drove forward by means of levers over the narrow neck of land across into the inner harbor. The Caesarian warships, which lay without crews tied up to the shore, were thus exposed to two converging attacks; and the enemy soon succeeded in hauling off four and in burning the remainder. With this successful issue to his raid, the younger Pompeius transferred Decimus Laelius from the Asiatic fleet, leaving him to continue the operations against the town; and under his supervision a strict blockade was maintained against all attempts to provision it from the two neighboring cities of Byllis and Amantia.

Pompeius himself went north to Alessio, where he attacked and burned inside the harbor of that city everyone of the thirty transports lately left there by Mark Antony. On endeavoring, however, to storm Alessio itself, he was met by such a stout resistance from the Roman citizens settled in the district, and by the regular troops whom Caesar had previously sent down as a garrison, that after three days spent in fruitless attempts at assault, in the course of which he suffered some slight casualties, he was obliged to withdraw his squadron with his object unattained.

Meanwhile Caesar also had continued his operations. With the definite intelligence that Pompeius was now established at Asparagium, he set his united army in motion for the same objective, merely breaking his march to storm the chief town of the Parthini, then in the hands of a Pompeian garrison. The third day brought him face to face with Pompeius; upon which he ordered his camp to be made in close proximity to his opponent, and on the morrow, advancing in full strength after completing his dispositions for battle, challenged his rival to a decisive combat. But it was soon evident that Pompeius was not to be enticed from his fortified lines, and Caesar had again to fall back upon camp, clearly recognizing that some alternative plan of action must now be tried. The next day, therefore, with the whole of his effective forces he commenced a wide turning movement to the eastwards, along a difficult and narrow road, with the object of marching directly upon Durazzo. Such a diversion, it was hoped, would either force Pompeius northwards upon that city, or, failing that, sever his communications with it; the latter alternative being no less desirable than the other was probable, since Durazzo was by far the most important food-dépôt and the principal place of arms in the hands of the enemy. Nor were his expectations disappointed. At first Pompeius failed to read the mind of his rival; for, on seeing the Caesarian army march out of their entrenchments by a route leading in an opposite direction to the northern emporium, he naturally concluded that want of supplies was responsible for this enforced departure. Later in the day he heard the real truth from his scouts; and the next morning, breaking up his encampment, he started in pursuit, in the hope that the shorter route would allow him to head off his opponent in time. Caesar, however, who had foreseen this contingency, now called upon his troops for a supreme effort. The march was barely interrupted throughout the night, and early the next morning his army arrived before Durazzo just as the vanguard of the Pompeians debouched into sight. Caesar then camped on his new position.

Pompeius' land communications with Durazzo (*Dyrrachium*) were thus severed; and finding his original design no longer practicable, he fell back upon the next best alternative open to him, and on the heights known as Petra, a site within fairly easy reach of ships, which can lie there under the lee of the wind when this is in certain quarters, fresh permanent fortifications were now erected. The command was also given for a portion of his naval force to concentrate at the new station; whilst provisions and supplies were ordered up from Asia Minor and other countries under his military control.

Such measures as these threatened to involve, in Caesar's judgment, an indefinite prolongation of the war. Besides, he already regarded as hopeless the supplies waiting for him across the water in Italy; so complete a blockade was maintained along the entire coast by the Pompeians, and so protracted was the delay of his own war-fleets built by his orders during the late winter in Sicily, Gaul, and Italy. The necessity of feeding his army thus forced him to turn to Epirus, to which country he accordingly dispatched Quintus Tillius and Lucius Canuleius, the latter a staff-officer, on a special commission for that purpose; while to deal with the difficulty arising from the excessive distance of these regions, a series of large granaries was established at fixed points, and a regular service of corn-transport allotted to each of the neighboring communities. Similar orders were given to collect from Alessio, and from the district of the Parthini and all the hill villages, all the corn to be found there. This proved a mere handful, and that for two reasons: the natural quality of the soil is unfavorable, the country being a wild mountainous tract relying mostly on imported grain; and, moreover, Pompeius had anticipated this movement of his opponent, and, treating the Parthini during the last few days as legitimate booty, had ordered all cereals to be collected and brought into his lines at Petra under an escort of cavalry, with powers to pillage and overturn the houses of the inhabitants.

Seeing the unpromising outlook of affairs, Caesar evolved a plan of operations based upon the actual conditions of the ground. The position held by Pompeius was encircled by numerous lofty and rugged hills. These he first of all secured with outpost detachments, which at once proceeded to fortify on each a strong redoubt; and then, upon their completion, a continuous chain of earthworks was extended along the lines of least natural resistance, thus linking up fort with fort, and the circumvallation of Pompeius was begun. A triple result was anticipated from the new movement. Weighing well the shortness of his own supplies and Pompeius' overwhelming superiority in cavalry, Caesar confidently expected that not only would convoys of food-stuffs and other material requirements for his army now be freer to approach from all quarters with less danger of attack, but the Pompeian cavalry would also be cut off from provender and so rendered

C₁ Caesar's Camp during Blockade. P₁ Pompey's Camp during Blockade.
C₂   ,,   ,,   after   ,,   P₂ ,,   ,,   after   ,,
M Camp of Marcellinus.   P. G. Postern Gate of Subsidiary Camp.

useless as a military force; and finally, he argued, a severe blow would thus be dealt to his opponent's prestige, a matter on which he notoriously placed most reliance in his intercourse with foreign states, when the news ran round the civilized world that the great commander was blockaded by Caesar and dare not face a pitched battle. And, indeed, Pompeius now found himself in a serious dilemma. He was unwilling to draw off from the sea and the neighborhood of Durazzo, since that town had been converted into an emporium for all his war material, including arms, accoutrements, and ordnance; whilst there was also the further objection that he depended entirely on sea-borne supplies for the feeding of his army. On the other hand, he was equally powerless to prevent the completion of Caesar's blockading lines, except by consenting to a general engagement; and that he had determined was not at the present juncture advisable. His sole remaining alternative was one which, considered as a military measure, amounted wellnigh to a counsel of despair. It consisted in occupying all the hills that he could seize, so that by enclosing in a ring of fortified posts the widest possible sweep of country, he might keep the Caesarian forces at such extreme distance as he could thus command. Nor did the event belie his expectations. Twenty-four outposts were soon completed, sufficient to encircle an arc some fifteen miles in extent: within this space his army's foraging then proceeded, and, as the area also contained within itself many hand-sown crops, the transport animals could for the present at any rate continue to subsist.

Meanwhile the two armies were busily entrenching one against the other. As fast as the Caesarians pushed their fortifications in an unbroken line from each redoubt on to the next, in order to prevent the Pompeians from breaking through at any point and so taking them in the rear; the enemy on the inner circle were also extending a parallel chain of works, likewise intended to prevent the possibility of their own line being pierced and themselves surrounded from behind. But in this contest of the spade it was soon clear the Pompeians were winning: the greater number of their sappers, and the shorter arc required on the inner side, rendered such a result inevitable. Moreover, whenever it became necessary for Caesar to occupy new positions in the progress of his works, Pompeius, without advancing in force to dispute them by a regular pitched battle, which he was resolved as yet to avoid, would nevertheless select his own ground, and constantly dispatch against us bodies of archers and slingers (an arm in which he was exceptionally strong), and by this device inflicted severe wounds upon our men. Indeed so great had grown the dread inspired by the enemy's arrows, that very nearly all the Caesarians had made themselves shirts or other coverings, of felt, or quilted padding, or hides, as a protection against these missiles.

In establishing themselves at the various outposts desperate struggles ensued on either side. While Caesar strove to hem in Pompeius within the narrowest boundaries possible, it was Pompeius' main object to occupy as many hills in as wide a circuit as he could control. Constant minor actions were thus fought solely from this reason, notably one in which the Ninth Caesarian legion was engaged. This corps had just seized a certain height and commenced fortifying it, when the Pompeians took possession of a second hill in close proximity to and directly confronting the other. Between the two there intervened at one point a fairly level causeway of communication. Accordingly Pompeius, after first throwing out flanking bodies of archers and slingers, pushed forward a strong force of light infantry, and then, bringing up his siege-guns, settled down to hamper the construction of our entrenchments. It was thus no light task for our soldiers at the same time to defend their position and also continue the work of fortification. Seeing his men, therefore, continually exposed to wounds from all sides, Caesar ordered their retreat, and the evacuation of the post. The retreat led down an incline, and the enemy, emboldened all the more to press home the attack, determined to render our withdrawal a difficult matter, convinced as they were that panic was responsible for the abandonment of the position. It was during this incident that Pompeius is credited with having addressed the boastful remark to his suite, that he was prepared to forfeit all claim to be considered a general of experience, if the Caesarian legions should succeed in extricating themselves from the consequences of their own ill-considered advance.

Meanwhile the dangers threatening the retreat caused Caesar considerable disquiet. The order was given to move up to the front a number of military hurdles, to be placed in position along the ridge of the hill in line of the attack: under cover of these the troops were then commanded to dig a moderately wide ditch on the near or inner side, and to render the whole ground as impracticable and difficult as possible. In addition, Caesar personally posted bodies of slingers at various strategic points, to lend further assistance to the retreat; then, with his precautions completed, he gave the order for the legion to be retired. This was at once the signal to the enemy for a still more determined and exultant advance; and, driving our men before them, they thrust aside the defenses formed by the interposing hurdles, preparatory to crossing the trenches. Seeing what was happening, and fearing the movement might be interpreted as not so much a retreat as a rout, leading to a still graver disaster to his arms, Caesar first sent his men a word of encouragement through Antonius, the officer commanding this legion, and then, from the troops' present position some halfway down the hill, ordered his trumpeter to sound the advance for a combined charge upon the enemy. With a sudden unanimous impulse, the men of the Ninth discharged their volley of heavy javelins; then breasting the hill at the double, from their lower ground they drove the Pompeians back in headlong flight, and compelled them to turn and run. Their flight, however, proved no easy matter, and they were greatly hampered by the opposing hurdles and long poles that blocked the way, and no less by the complex lines of intersecting ditches. As to our own troops, they considered their object fully attained if they could withdraw without serious damage. Having, therefore, inflicted severe losses upon the enemy, at a cost to themselves of only five casualties, they completed their retirement in perfect safety, and subsequently occupying another series of hills, a little outside the previous line, finished off the work of circumvallation.

Strange, indeed, and altogether unparalleled in military history was the character of the present operations. The great number of the redoubts, the wide extent of country covered, the long undulating lines of entrenchment, in a word, the whole nature of the blockade, all doubtless contributed to such a result, but they were not the only causes. Other generals have before now endeavored to blockade an opponent; but it has always been as the sequel to an attack upon a broken and stricken enemy, either suffering under some defeat in battle, or demoralized by some other piece of misfortune. As a further contrast, the side which has thus invested the other could invariably count a superiority both in infantry and mounted troops, and their object has usually been the interruption of the enemy's supplies. Yet here was Caesar endeavoring with an army numerically inferior to encircle an opponent whose strength was as yet unimpaired either by material or moral disaster, and who possessed in addition an abundance of all military stores. Everyday ships were arriving from every quarter of the Empire, expressly chartered to carry supplies; and the wind could not blow from any point of the compass without some of their number having a fair run for their voyage. In marked opposition to all this, Caesar had already eaten up every vestige of corn that the length and breadth of the country could provide, and was now in most desperate straits. Yet his men set themselves to endure their privations with exemplary fortitude. They were cheered by the recollection of their similar hardships a year ago in Spain, when their long-suffering efforts were rewarded by the successful termination of a great war: they remembered likewise the slender nature of their rations before Alesia, rations which were still further reduced at Avaricum,[11] and yet from both these critical positions they had emerged victorious over the most powerful combinations of tribes. They were not the men therefore to reject either the barley or the pulse which was now served out to them; while as to animal food, of which there was plenty in Epirus, they regarded it as a positive luxury. A lucky discovery was also made by those who had lately been responsible for the vegetable supplies[12] of the army, who now found a species of wild root called Chara. This, when mixed with milk, did much to alleviate the distress: it was made up like bread, and there was no lack of its supply. Indeed, in some of the informal conversations which passed between the private soldiers of the hostile camps, in which the Pompeians taunted our men with their starved condition, the latter's usual answer was to toss these loaves across at their opponents as the best way of dashing their rising hopes.[13]

But now the corn crops were beginning to ripen, and mere hope was enough to sustain the empty stomachs of the troops with its assurance of rapidly approaching plenty. Alike on picket duty and in the quiet talk amongst comrades, constant expressions of the dominant temper of the men were heard, that they would sooner live on the bark of trees than allow Pompeius to slip from their grasp. Much satisfaction was also caused by the reports brought in by deserters, who declared that though the troop-horses were still kept alive all other transport animals had perished. They added that the army itself enjoyed but indifferent health. Not only were they cooped up in the narrowest of quarters, exposed to the foul stench of hundreds of putrifying bodies, but they were quite unfit for the continual fatigue duty now required of them, and, worst of all, they suffered acutely from scarcity of water. This last hardship was due to the direct action of Caesar himself, who had either diverted or else dammed with solid obstructions every river or rivulet whose course led down to the sea. For the district being a mountainous one, and the valleys converging so narrowly as to form as it were natural conduits, it was easy to block such channels by cross-rows of piles let into the ground, which, when strengthened by artificial mounds, effectually held up the water. In consequence, the Pompeians were compelled of sheer necessity to search, along the lower ground where it was swampy, and to dig wells there, thus adding one more task to their daily round of labors. And yet, even when found, such sources of water had the marked disadvantage of being a considerable distance from some of the outposts, and, further, they quickly dried up under the sultry heat of summer. On the other hand, Caesar's army enjoyed not only perfect health but a water supply that was practically unlimited; whilst, with the sole exception of wheat, there were stores in abundance of every description; and even in this particular, the soldiers of Pompeius had the mortification of daily seeing a better time coming for their adversaries, and their hopes rising under the prospect of the ripening corn.

So unexampled a type of warfare naturally called forth equally curious stratagems on either side. For example, the Pompeians, having noticed from the campfires that our regiments lay out at night on their entrenchments, would steal out silently to the attack, and, after discharging a volley of arrows into our crowded lines, would swiftly rejoin their main body. To remedy this annoyance, our people learnt by experience to light their fires in one place (and to pass the night in another).[14]

* * * * * * * * * * * * * *

Meanwhile intelligence of the critical position of the battalion reached Publius Sulla, the officer left in command of the camp by Caesar when marching out to the attack. He at once went to the rescue with a force of two legions, his arrival causing the easy repulse of the Pompeians. Without waiting to face the Caesarian infantry or to stand their charge, the main body turned their backs and abandoned their position as soon as ever the leading companies were driven in. In the midst of the pursuit, and to stay our further advance, Sulla ordered the recall. Yet there is a strong consensus of opinion that, had he only allowed the pursuit to be pressed home with greater vigor, that day might have seen the termination of the war.

Such criticism on that officer's judgment can scarcely be maintained. The functions of a subordinate are not those of a commander-in-chief. The actions of the one should in all points be regulated by his instructions: the other is free to embrace in the scope of his plans the entire military situation. In this particular instance, Sulla had been deputed by Caesar to hold the camp in his own absence. Having, therefore, effected the relief of his companions-in-arms, he was content to rest upon that achievement: he was not prepared to take the further responsibility of fighting a general engagement with the enemy (which after all, he felt, might easily involve some disaster), lest his conduct should be interpreted as trenching on the province of his commander. His appearance on the scene of action, however, brought considerable difficulties to the retreating Pompeians. Their original advance had been upwards from a lower level, and they had subsequently occupied the crest of the hill. By withdrawing, therefore, down the slope, they were menaced with a pursuit that had all the advantages of position on its side; moreover, only a brief interval of daylight remained before sundown, since the hope of reaching a definite decision had made them carry the affair well on towards night. The force of circumstances thus impelled Pompeius, by a plan improvised at the moment, to seize a neighboring height just out of range of artillery fire from our redoubt; where after establishing himself and throwing up entrenchments, he proceeded to concentrate the whole of his effective forces.

At the same time fighting also took place in two other parts of the field, since Pompeius had supported his main attack by subsidiary movements against a number of our redoubts, with the object of dividing the defense and so preventing the dispatch of reinforcements from the neighboring outposts. Thus at one point Volcatius Tullus successfully withstood the assault of an entire legion of Pompeians, and, taking the offensive, actually drove it from its ground; at another, the German auxiliaries sallied out from our lines, and after accounting for a considerable number of the enemy, safely effected their retirement back to their supports. On this day, therefore, six distinct engagements were fought, viz. three outside Durazzo and three up at the trenches. Upon our investigating the total casualties for the day, it was found that of the Pompeians no fewer than two thousand had fallen—mostly reservists and centurions—included in the number being Valerius Flaccus, son of Lucius Flaccus, sometime governor of the Province of Asia Minor. Of regimental and company colors six altogether were brought in. On our side the killed amounted to no more than twenty in all six battles, though, on the other hand, of the men inside the redoubt not one escaped unwounded, and of the company officers[15] belonging to this one battalion four out of the six had lost their eyes. When the garrison wanted to adduce evidence of the desperate nature of their struggle, they collected the arrows which had been shot into the fort and counted out before Caesar some thirty thousand; and, on the shield of the centurion Scaeva being brought up for inspection, it was found pierced with a hundred-and-twenty separate holes. As some reward for this man's gallant services both to himself and the country he so well represented, Caesar first presented him with a purse of £1,500, and then publicly announced his promotion from the eighth to the first battalion of the legion, and to the senior company in that; it being common testimony that the successful defense of the redoubt had been largely owing to his splendid exertions. The whole battalion subsequently received double pay and rations, and was also richly rewarded by Caesar with gifts of new uniform and various decorations for distinguished conduct in the field.

Meanwhile Pompeius had employed the night in making large additions to his defenses; on the following days these were strengthened by a series of military towers, and when the works had been carried to a height of fifteen feet, this face of the camp was screened by a number of portable shelters; five days after that another moderately cloudy night again lent him its friendly assistance. Orders were at once given to barricade all the camp gates, which were then left as a check to pursuit; and in the early hours of the morning the Pompeian forces silently evacuated the hill and fell back upon their old entrenchments. Upon the next and upon each succeeding day Caesar marched out with his army to form up for action where the ground was level, in hopes that he might find Pompeius ready to give decisive battle. In executing this movement he so disposed his legions that they were virtually commanded by the Pompeian camp, his front line being so close to the enemy's rampart that it only just cleared the range of hand-missiles and artillery. To disregard so direct a challenge was obviously impossible if Pompeius was to retain his military reputation and prestige. The Pompeian army was therefore drawn up outside its entrenchments, but in such a formation that its rearmost line actually abutted on the breastworks, while the whole of the force thus embattled could be effectually covered by the fire from its own ramparts.

The success gained by Cassius Longinus and Calvisius Sabinus in securing the adhesion of Livadia (*Aetolia*), and the country round the Gulf of Arta (*Acarnania* and *Amphilochia*), by the steps already indicated,[16] now led Caesar to believe that the time was ripe for a similar movement with regard to Greece proper (*Achaea*), which would carry the range of his arms over a somewhat wider area. Quintus Fufius Calenus was accordingly sent into that country, and Sabinus and Cassius, with the forces under them, were subordinated to his command. Rutilius Lupus was at this time acting as governor of Greece, in virtue of his appointment by Pompeius; and he, on receiving intelligence of the advance of the three Caesarian generals, at once took measures for the fortification of the Isthmus, so as to form some barrier between Fufius and the Peloponnese. Calenus meanwhile took over the submission voluntarily tendered by the local authorities, of Delphi, Thebes, and Orchomenus; other cities were taken by storm, and for the remainder, active steps were inaugurated for winning them over to the Caesarian interest through special missions dispatched for that purpose. These and similar duties served to engross the attention of Fufius.

Whilst the above events were passing in Greece (*Achaea*) and the neighborhood of Durazzo, as soon as the news of Scipio's arrival in Macedonia was fully confirmed, Caesar, loath to abandon his traditional policy, directed Aulus Clodius to proceed on an embassy to the camp of the new commander. Clodius had the advantage of being a common friend to both parties, as he had originally been introduced by Scipio to the notice of Caesar, who had since made it a special point to treat him as one of his own intimates. Caesar now entrusted him with a letter addressed to Scipio, supplementing it by verbal instructions of which the following formed a summary.

In spite of all his efforts in the direction of peace, nothing tangible had yet been effected, chiefly owing, as he was disposed to think, to the supineness of those whom he had chosen as his intermediaries, who shrank from the task of conveying his terms to Pompeius at a time when they would be unacceptable. Scipio, on the other hand, possessed an authority with his chief that not only enabled him to speak his mind freely on all subjects, but to a large extent gave him also the right of criticism and of rectifying the blunders of his colleague; moreover, he held an independent command in the field, and was thus able to back his authority by a military force that could compel obedience. If he were now to take this step, he would win from the world the unanimous tribute of being the one man who had given rest to a distracted Italy and peace to the provinces, and in so doing saved the Empire from disruption.

These instructions Clodius duly carried to Scipio, and for the first few days apparently met with a favorable hearing; later on he was not admitted to further conference, the reason being, as we afterwards discovered on conclusion of the war, that Scipio had been roundly taken to task for his weakness by Favonius. The negotiations thus proved abortive, and Clodius had no alternative but to return to Caesar.

CHAPTER FOUR

THE FORCING OF THE BLOCKADE

IT WAS ESSENTIAL TO CAESAR'S PLAN THAT THE POMPEIAN CAVALRY should be closely confined in Durazzo, and not allowed any opportunity of procuring forage. Accordingly he proceeded to draw across the two approaches to the town which, as already stated,[1] were not wide, strong lines of entrenched works supported by redoubts. This new movement quickly convinced Pompeius that no serious diversion could be expected from his horse; and after a few days it was put on board ship and brought back within his permanent lines.

The want of fodder continued to make itself acutely felt: so hard pressed indeed were they, that the horses had to be fed on leaves torn from the trees, varied by a mash made from the succulent roots of reeds; for as for the young corn which they had found already sown within their lines, that had all long been eaten up. Thus they were obliged to import fodder from Corfu and Arta (*Acarnania*), a course involving a long sea-voyage, and even then the supply was so scanty that it had to be eked out with barley in order to keep the animals alive. At last there came a time when every locality had alike been stripped of barley, fodder, and all other vegetation whatever, and when even the foliage from the trees began to run out; and when this point of destitution was reached, Pompeius, with his cavalry mounts reduced to skeletons and rendered totally unfit for active service, at length decided that some attempt must be made towards forcing the blockade.

Now there were serving with Caesar on the roll of the cavalry two brother Allobroges, Roucillus and Egus, sons of Adbucillus, for many years the paramount chief of his tribe, two men whose services to Caesar all through the Gallic wars had been marked no less by gallantry than efficiency. In return for this loyal support Caesar had appointed them to the highest magistracies in their own country, had contrived their election to the tribal Senate without passing through the usual grades, had given them not only lands captured from the enemy during the war but also large sums of ready money, and in a word, had raised them from poverty to affluence. Their personal courage had not only won them a warm place in Caesar's own regard, but with the army in general they were also great favorites. Unfortunately they allowed their friendship with Caesar to foster a pride that was as foolish as it is characteristic of subject races, and from despising their Gallic companion-in-arms, they came to cheating them of their pay, and even went so far as to appropriate the whole share of the plunder that should have fallen to their men. Exasperated by such injustice, the troopers in a body waited upon Caesar, and loudly complained of their leaders' fraud; adding to their other charges the further accusation that false returns were habitually made of the cavalry's strength, in order that the brothers might pocket the extra pay.

Caesar, considering present circumstances to be unfavorable for the visitation of punishment, and ready to forgive much to a gallant soldier, decided to postpone the whole inquiry: nevertheless, he privately censured the two chieftains for making money out of their troop, and after a reminder that there was no limit to the power of his friendship, advised them to gauge his future kindness to themselves on the basis of that already experienced at his hands. In spite of this secrecy, the affair caused a popular outburst of bitter and contemptuous feeling towards the two brothers, the reality of which was brought home to their notice, as much by their own inward self-condemnation and accusing voice of conscience, as by the open taunts levelled at them from outside. Deeply resenting their humiliation, and, it may be, convinced in their own minds that instead of being given their acquittal they were only reserved for future punishment, they determined to sever their connection with us and our party, and to seek their fortunes in another camp, and make new friendships there. Having, therefore, communicated their design to a few intimate dependants, whom they dared trust with so desperate a venture, they first of all endeavored to murder the cavalry brigadier, Caius Volusenus (a fact only discovered afterwards at the close of the war), as some earnest of sincerity in their treacherous desertion to Pompeius; and when the difficulties of this project proved insurmountable and no opportunity presented itself of carrying it into effect, they proceeded to borrow all the ready money they could, under the appearance of desiring to do satisfaction to their fellow countrymen and restore their fraudulent gains, and then, buying up a large batch of horses, they went over to Pompeius, followed by those who were privy to the plot. Arrived in Pompeius' camp, they were received in a manner befitting their own exalted rank and liberal education. Pompeius indeed could not but take into account the fact that a considerable retinue had accompanied their arrival, and that numerous remounts had been also added to his army. The men were of acknowledged gallantry, who, until recently, had been held in high reputation by Caesar; and the very unexpectedness of their present exploit was itself some justification for Pompeius' action.

In consideration of all this, the two chiefs were conducted in person by Pompeius on a tour of inspection round his lines, where every detail was pointed out to them. For till now not a single foot soldier or cavalryman had gone over from Caesar to his rival, though the desertions from Pompeius' camp were of almost daily occurrence; whilst the troops which had been raised in Epirus and Livadia (*Aetolia*) and in all the regions now under the military control of Caesar commonly went over *en masse*. Now, however, deserters had arrived who knew every secret of the enemy: the unfinished portions of his siege lines, the additional touches of strength desired at certain places by the engineering experts, the regular routine of duties amongst the besiegers, the distances between point and point, the varying degrees of watchfulness among the different pickets according to the natural temperament or zeal of the respective officers in charge—all this they had seen and noted, and no less a gift than this they now imparted to Pompeius.

That commander first made himself thoroughly master of their detailed information, and then, having already, as mentioned above, formed the design of a sortie, issued orders to his troops to make wicker coverings for their helmets, and to provide themselves with a quantity of entrenching soil. These preparations completed, at nightfall a strong body of light infantry and archers was embarked on board dinghies and galley-oared transports, and shortly after midnight a force of sixty battalions drawn from both the main camp and the strongest outposts, was put under motion for that section of the circumvallating lines which abutted on the sea and which was furthest removed from Caesar's own head quarters. The same rendezvous was given to the fleet of vessels which had been loaded, as described, with their freight of earth and light infantrymen, and at the same time the Pompeian battleships were brought round from Durazzo. After this each officer was carefully instructed as to his own share in the forthcoming operations.

At this particular corner of the works Caesar had the Ninth legion in position, under command of his paymaster Lentulus Marcellinus; though owing to that officer's indifferent state of health Fulvius Postumus had been attached as his second in command. The works at this point were of the following design. First came a ditch fifteen feet wide; this was surmounted by a palisaded rampart ten feet high, facing the enemy, and backed by an equal depth of solid earth: then 200 yards in the rear rose a second and similar rampart, though of somewhat slighter proportions, and this time fronting outwards or in an opposite direction to the first. The reason for this double line was the apprehension disturbing Caesar's mind during the last few days that his position might here be turned by an approach from sea; and he therefore had to devise some means of defense in the event of his being exposed to a simultaneous assault from north and south. Unfortunately there had not been time to complete the scheme: the general scale of the works undertaken had been too vast, and the labor required for the seventeen miles circuit of entrenchments too incessant: consequently the cross-rampart which was to connect the two main lines, and had its front to the sea, was not yet finished off. This fact was well known to Pompeius through the information brought by the two treacherous Allobroges, and now became the cause of a considerable disaster to our arms. For soon after detachments of the Ninth had taken up their bivouac for the night in close proximity to the sea, the Pompeians were suddenly seen advancing in the grey light of early dawn. Their attack quickly developed itself from both sides. While the troops who had come by boat were pouring in a hot fire of missiles upon the outer or southern rampart, under cover of which the ditches were rapidly filled up with the earth brought for that purpose, the infantry of the legions were bringing up scaling ladders and creating no small confusion among the defenders on the inner stockade by volleys of artillery shot and hand-spears of all descriptions; whilst, to crown the disorder, swarms of archers were deploying in support of each of the two attacking bodies. What rendered matters worse was that our men had nothing to reply with excepting stones from their slings, and against such blows the enemy were largely protected by the wicker coverings previously fitted to their helmets. In the midst of this fierce onslaught, when resistance was already a desperate matter, the fatal discovery was made of the flaw in the fortifications already mentioned: troops were rapidly landed from the sea in boats at a point between the two parallel ramps where the works were still unfinished, and, taking our men in the rear, drove them from both lines and compelled them to turn and run.

As soon as information of this raid reached Marcellinus, that officer at once pushed up fresh battalions from camp to the support of his hard-pressed detachment. The sight of their comrades in full flight, however, was too much for his reserves; they could neither stay the stampede by their own arrival on the scene, nor did they attempt to stand against the onset of the enemy. As fast as the relieving columns followed one another, each and all caught the infection of panic from the fugitives, and thereby only added to the general confusion and critical position of the entire force, since the retreat threatened to become blocked though the heavy congestion of men.

While the battle was at its height the standard-bearer of the legion's eagle was mortally wounded; but just as his strength was failing the man caught sight of our passing cavalry. "Take this," said he, "which for many a year I have jealously guarded whilst living, and now that I'm dying hand back to Caesar with the self-same devotion: see to it, I charge you, that no negligence of yours bring about a military disgrace which was never yet known in the army of Caesar, but carry the standard back safe into his hands." By this fortunate incident the regimental colors were saved from capture, after the first battalion had lost everyone of its company commanders except the third in order of rank.

Meanwhile the victorious Pompeians were marching on the camp of Marcellinus, dealing out as they advanced heavy slaughter through our ranks. Their approach raised no little panic among the remaining battalions of the Ninth, until Marcus Antonius, who held the neighboring command in the line of redoubts, and who had been informed of the perilous nature of the position, was seen to be descending, with the hills behind him, at the head of a strong reliev-ing column of twelve battalions. His arrival on the field of action effectually checked the advancing enemy, and at the same time lent sufficient steadiness to the remaining troops to recover from their recent state of abject terror. Very soon afterwards Caesar himself arrived on the scene, accompanied by a few battalions, which he had rapidly drafted from the various outposts, on seeing the signal of rising smoke passed on from fort to fort, in accordance with the established custom of the preceding days. Realizing at once the extent of the disaster and perceiving that Pompeius had succeeded in forcing his way outside the lines of circumvallation, in such a manner that his foraging could be freely conducted along the seaboard whilst he still maintained communication with his ships, Caesar decided on a total revolution in the conduct of the war; and, his original plan having now miscarried, he gave orders to entrench a camp close up to the enemy's new position.

The work of fortification was just completed when his scouts dis-covered a large body of men, representing perhaps the strength of a legion, hidden behind a neighboring wood, on their march to what was known as the old camp. The situation of this camp was as follows. It had originally formed the head quarters of the Ninth legion, at the time when that regiment was ordered to stem the advance of the

Pompeians in this quarter, preparatory to walling them round in
the manner previously described; it rested upon a wood on one side,
and was not more than 500 yards from the sea. Subsequently, certain
reasons had produced a modification of plan, and Caesar had withdrawn this corps a little further inland. After a few days' interval, the
camp had been occupied by Pompeius himself; and as he intended
to post more than one legion at this particular point, the inner walls
were left standing and the main circuit greatly increased, the effect
being to convert the smaller camp thus contained by the larger into
a kind of fortified citadel to the other. A further change introduced
was to run a breastwork from the left-hand corner of the extended
lines down to the river bank, in order that the troops might water
with more freedom and without fear of molestation from the enemy.
But Pompeius too had changed his plans, for reasons unnecessary
here to particularize, and had evacuated the position; thus the camp
had existed for a considerable number of days, and all its fortifications were still intact.[2]

This was the site towards which our scouts now reported the
Pompeian legion to have headed, and the same movement was also
observed from some of our higher redoubts, which at once confirmed
the news. Now the place was distant from Pompeius' new camp about
800 yards. Caesar thereupon conceived the hope of successfully
crushing this isolated regiment; and being anxious to repair the day's
disaster, ordered two of his battalions to remain on the earthwork
and keep up the appearance of entrenching, whilst with the other
thirty-three, among which were those of the battered Ninth with its
heavy death-roll of officers[3] and sorely attenuated ranks, he marched
out with all the secrecy possible, in double column formation and
by a route pointing directly away from his objective, towards the
detached body of Pompeians and this lesser camp of theirs. Nor was
his judgment found to be at fault. Arriving safely at his destination
before Pompeius could become aware of his departure, he quickly
turned his left wing, where he himself was posted, against the enemy,
and, in spite of the formidable nature of the defenses, drove him
from the rampart. The camp gates proved to be blocked by *chevaux de
frise*, which slightly delayed our advance; and a sharp struggle ensued

between the impetuous efforts of our men to rush the obstacles and the stubborn resistance of the garrison; conspicuous amongst whom was Titus Puleio, who has been previously mentioned as responsible for the treacherous surrender of the army under Caius Antonius, and who now fought most gallantly from his place in the ranks. Our men, however, quickly asserted their superiority, and having hewn away the intervening barrier, burst first of all into the larger or outer camp, and from thence into the inner fortress contained in it, whither the defeated legion had retired, and where several were now cut down while still maintaining their resistance.

But, alas, there is a power which, mighty though it be in other spheres, is mightiest of all in war, working most momentous changes by means of incidents most trivial—we mean the power of Fortune: as was now to be exemplified. For the units composing the right Caesarian wing, in their ignorance of the ground, followed the course of the outlying breastwork, which ran, as already indicated, from the camp to the river side, searching for its gate and believing it to form the rampart to the main camp. On discovering their mistake, however, and finding it to be connected directly with the stream, they tore down the defenses and passed through without opposition, being followed by the whole body of mounted troops.

In the meanwhile, after this sufficiently serious delay, news of the attack reached the ears of Pompeius. He at once recalled five of his legions from their work on his new entrenchments, and advanced at their head to the relief of his beleaguered detachment; and while his cavalry bore down upon our troopers, our infantry on the rampart of the newly conquered camp discovered to their amazement a line of legionaries in full battle formation. In a moment the situation was completely altered. The isolated legion of Pompeians, rallying under the prospect of immediate relief, endeavored to make a stand at the postern gate, and even delivered a counter-attack upon our troops: Caesar's horse, at that moment engaged in scaling the outer breastwork through the narrow breaches, grew alarmed for the safety of its retreat, and gave the signal for general flight; whereupon the right wing, which had by this time lost touch with its left, seeing the panic pervading the mounted troops, and anxious to save itself from being crushed on the inner side of the earthwork, drew back again through the breaches which they had just made in it. There the greater part of them, afraid of being caught in the narrow gangways, hurled themselves over into the trenches of a rampart fully ten feet high; the first of them were trampled to death, but the rest passed out into safety over the dead bodies of their comrades. Similarly on the left wing, as soon as the Caesarians saw from their station on the rampart that the Pompeian army was upon them, and their own second division in headlong flight, a dread arose of finding themselves completely trapped in the narrow interval, now that they had an enemy both inside and outside the rampart; and they began looking to their own safety by retracing the steps of their previous advance. Everywhere alike was confusion and panic-stricken flight, so utterly uncontrolled that when Caesar snatched at the standards of some of the fugitives and ordered the men to halt, some let go their horses and joined in the stampede on foot, while others were so beside themselves with terror as to let even the standards go, and not a single man could be induced to stand his ground.

Disastrous as the situation was, there were still some redeeming circumstances, without which the total annihilation of the army must inevitably have followed. Foremost among these was Pompeius' fear of ambush, due in all probability to his astonishment at the turn events had taken, after he had just seen his own men chased out of their entrenchments; an astonishment which now rendered him for sometime nervous about approaching the outer works: and another advantage was that, the camp gates being narrow and firmly held by Caesar's troops, the pursuit of the cavalry was thereby considerably delayed. Thus it happened that the same circumstance, trivial in itself, produced two quite dissimilar trains of consequences, each of them far-reaching in its effects. It was the breastwork leading from camp to the river that, at the moment when the Pompeian lines had been carried, intervened between Caesar and a victory as good as won: it was the same obstacle which now, by retarding the enemy's pursuit, proved in turn the salvation of our force.[4]

These two battles on this one day cost Caesar altogether 960 of the rank and file, besides the distinguished Roman knights Tuticanus

Gallus, son of a Roman senator, Caius Fleginas of Piacenza (*Placentia*), Aulus Granius of Pozzuoli (*Puteoli*), and Marcus Sacrativer of Capua, as well as thirty-two regimental and company officers. A large proportion, however, of these met their death either by suffocation in the trenches, or at the narrow gaps in the earthworks, or down by the river banks, without the infliction of any sort of wound, and merely through the terrorized flight of their own comrades. Of military standards thirty-two in all were lost.

As a result of the day's fighting Pompeius was formally acclaimed "Commander" by his troops, a name which he retained, and subsequently allowed himself to be addressed by, although he rarely used the title at the head of his official dispatches, and never wore the usual laurel wreath on the staves of his military attendants.[5] In marked contrast to this moderation was the conduct of Labienus. Having induced his chief to order the transfer of the prisoners to his own charge, he first had them marched on to the parade ground, presumably for the sake of display and to strengthen people's faith in a traitor, and then addressing them as fellow soldiers, and asking in terms of studied insult whether veteran troops were in the habit of running away, butchered the whole body in cold blood before the eyes of the assembled army.

These successes evoked such overweening confidence in the camp of the Pompeians, that, disdaining all further thought for the conduct of the war, they regarded the campaign as already won. They did not pause to consider the weakness of our own force, or the adverse conditions and cramped dimensions of the late battlefield, due to the enemy's previous possession of the camp; so that, face which way we would, we had to meet a double menace both from within and without the rampart. They failed to take account of the circumstance that our army had been cut into two halves, neither of which could help the other; nor did they make the further reflection that the action had not been the result of a fair charge in open fight, but that our self-inflicted losses from the overcrowding and want of room had been even heavier than those inflicted by the enemy. Finally, they forgot to allow for the ordinary vicissitudes of war, and for the numerous occasions on which the most trivial incidents have been the cause of the gravest disasters—for example, an ill-grounded suspicion, a sudden panic, or a superstitious scruple—and the frequency with which an army in the field has come to grief through either an inefficient general or a careless subordinate. All this they now ignored, and acting as though they had won solely on their merits, and no further change of fortune were possible, they began, both by word of mouth and written dispatch, to fill the entire world with a chorus of jubilation over the victory this day had brought them.

Meanwhile the position of Caesar, after the overthrow of his earlier designs, rendered it advisable in his judgment to make a complete revolution in his conduct of the war. He first withdrew at one stroke everyone of the garrisons in his chain of redoubts, and definitely abandoned the blockade. He then called up the whole force and publicly harangued the men, urging them not to take too much to heart their recent misfortunes or be alarmed at what had occurred, but pointing out the unreasonableness of setting against their long line of victories in the past a single reverse which was after all an insignificant one.

On the contrary, they owed much thanks to Fortune. Italy had been won by them without a scratch; the two Spains with their teeming population of fighting races, led by generals of the highest skill and military experience, had been reduced to peace and order; the home provinces, on whose corn they depended, had been brought under effective occupation; while to crown the series of successes, there was the astonishing piece of good fortune which enabled them all to cross the water in perfect safety through the very center of the enemy's fleets, who swarmed alike before the harbors and along the open coastline. If their run of luck had not proved absolutely unbroken, they must remember that heaven helps those who help themselves. As far as he personally was concerned in their late disaster, he was the last man who could be justly held responsible. He had provided a fair field for the encounter; the enemy's camp had been captured, the enemy himself turned out of his entrenchments, and all opposition overcome.

Whatever it was that had then stepped in to snatch victory from his grasp—whether some unsteadiness of their own, somebody's blunder, or even the fickleness of Fortune—at the very moment when victory lay assured in their hands; at all events every man must now earnestly strive to atone for that regrettable incident by his own good conduct in the future. That would convert their defeat into a blessing, as had once before been the case at Gergovia;[6] and they who had lately shrank from a conflict would become the first to throw down the challenge.

At the close of this speech a sentence of public disgrace was passed upon certain of the standard-bearers, who were forthwith relieved of their position of trust. Through the army generally such burning indignation arose at the thought of their late discomfiture, and so fierce a longing to retrieve the tarnished reputation of their arms, that without waiting for the word of command from battalion or company officers, the men of their own accord even added to their ordinary duties by way of punishment; and such a burning desire to meet the enemy pervaded all ranks, that even higher-grade officers were found seriously persuading themselves that they ought to hold on to their present position and risk the chances of a general engagement.

Against all such views, Caesar felt the danger of trusting troops which had so recently yielded to panic, and thought it wiser to allow them time sufficient to recover their confidence: moreover, with the raising of the blockade, the question of his supplies had become acute. No time was therefore lost beyond what was required for attending to the sick and wounded, and at nightfall the baggage-trains of the army were all quietly got under motion and dispatched on the road to Apollonia, with strict orders to make no halt whatever before completing their full day's march. They were accompanied by an escort of one legion. These preliminaries satisfactorily disposed of, at about three o'clock in the morning two other legions were told off to remain in camp, while the rest of the force moved out by a number of separate gates, and were likewise dispatched on the same journey. Last of all, after another brief interval, in order that military tradition might be maintained and yet his own departure be disclosed at the latest possible moment, Caesar gave the word for the march to be openly sounded; and his rearguard turning out at once, quickly overhauled the preceding column, and was soon out of sight of their old entrenchments.

Equally little delay in the pursuit was observed by Pompeius when once he had divined his adversary's purpose; but acting on the lines that Caesar had foreseen, viz. to seize the opportunity of catching his enemy in the general panic which must follow, he conceived, on the disorganization of the march, he drew out his army from camp, and at once detached his cavalry to harass the retreat of the rearguard. This, however, they failed to overtake, since Caesar, by marching light, had gained a long start of his pursuers. But on reaching the river Schkumbi (*Genusus*), the awkward banks of this stream gave time for the Pompeian horsemen to come up, and an endeavor was made to delay the rearmost divisions by forcing an engagement. Against this attack Caesar opposed his own cavalry, interspersing through the squadrons a body of four hundred front rank legionaries lightly equipped; and so well did these perform in the ensuing cavalry action, that they totally routed the Pompeians, and after killing a large number, rejoined the column without any loss to themselves.[7]

The army of Caesar had now completed a full day's march, in accordance with his pre-arranged plan, and after safely making the passage of the Schkumbi (*Genusus*), took up its quarters in its old lines fronting Asparagium. The infantry of the legions were confined strictly to camp; the cavalry were first sent out to give the impression of foraging, and then ordered to return with all speed by the rearmost gate that was out of sight of the enemy. Meanwhile Pompeius had also completed a full day's march, and he too from similar motives decided to occupy his old position at Asparagium. The fortifications of this were still intact, and the troops, being thus relieved from their ordinary duty of entrenchment, began straying some distance from camp, partly after firewood, partly in quest of fodder, whilst others were seen leaving the rampart in the direction of their late camping-ground. The explanation of this last circumstance was that the decision to march having been taken hastily, a large proportion of the army's baggage and soldiers' kits had been left behind; and it was to recover this lost property that the troops, tempted by the nearness of the camp they had just evacuated, now strayed off from the trenches, after first discarding their arms and depositing them in their tents. As soon as they had thus incapacitated themselves for pursuit, Caesar, who had foreseen this very result, gave the signal for departure, it being then about midday; and his army, moving out of camp once more for a second march on the same day, proceeded to cover an additional eight miles from that spot; it being impossible for Pompeius to do the same on account of the straying of his troops.

The next day the same order was observed, and with the first fall of night the transport was again sent on in advance, to be followed about 3 AM by the main force under the personal direction of Caesar, who thus made sure that, if compelled to fight, he should be in a position to meet the sudden emergency with his army free of encumbrances. Throughout the following days the same dispositions were repeated; and as a result of these precautions the retreat was conducted without hitch or accident of any kind, in spite of having to traverse rivers of great depth and country exceptionally difficult. For Pompeius never recovered the time lost on the first day. Strive as he would to accelerate by forced marches the pace of his army, in his eagerness to overtake those ahead of him, his efforts were all in vain; on the fourth day he abandoned the pursuit, and recognized the necessity of some alternative plan of action. As for Caesar, various reasons had concurred in forcing him to touch at Apollonia. There were the wounded to be provided for, the army to be paid, the local communities to be reassured, garrisons to be stationed in the principal towns. The time allotted to these matters, however, was no more than the urgency of his situation made necessary: all his thoughts were riveted on Domitius, and the risk he ran of being caught by the Pompeian advance before he himself could get up with him; and he was now pressing towards that officer with all the speed which deep concern for his peril could elicit.

Considered in its general bearings, the scheme of operations which it was his purpose to develop rested on the following calculations. If Pompeius were making for the same point as himself, then he would be drawing his enemy away from the sea and from all the reserve supplies accumulated by him at Durazzo: Pompeius could then be forced to fight out the issue on equal terms, deprived of the support of his food stocks and other military stores. Supposing, on the other hand, Pompeius decided to cross into Italy,[8] it would then be easy for himself to effect a junction with Domitius, and to march his army round the head of the Adriatic to the relief of that country. Finally, if his opponent attempted to lay siege to Apollonia and Oricum, with the object of cutting all Caesar's communications with the coast, he would find himself confronted with the blockade of Scipio and the imperative necessity of going to the relief of his isolated force. Reasoning on these lines he forthwith dispatched couriers in advance to Cnaeus Domitius, with written instructions indicating the course of action that officer was to pursue; and after establishing garrisons at Apollonia, Alessio (*Lissus*), and Oricum of four, one, and three battalions respectively, and after carefully housing his wounded, he started on his march through Epirus and the region of Athamania.[9]

During this same time Pompeius was hastening towards the same goal. Conjectural interpretation of Caesar's motives pointed to a rapid movement towards Scipio as the soundest strategy of the moment. Should Caesar and himself take the same line, he could then reinforce his lieutenant; or, if he proved unwilling to quit the seaboard and the neighborhood of Oricum, through continued hopes of fresh legions and cavalry from Italy, the way would thus be open to himself to fall upon Domitius with the whole of his effective strength. Speed, therefore, was now the first consideration on both sides; each had the twofold object of rescuing their friends and of seizing the rare opportunity offered by the present conjunction of events for crushing an opponent. But whereas Caesar was going out of his way in touching at Apollonia, Pompeius had a clear road before him into Macedonia through the Candavian tract;[10] and a further complication had now arisen from an altogether unforeseen event. This was disposition of Domitius, who, after lying encamped for several days cheek by jowl with Scipio, had been compelled by want of supplies to vacate his watch upon that general, and to retire in the direction of Heraclia;[11]

and as that town lies at the foot of the Candavian hill country, it seemed as though Fortune herself were conspiring to throw him across the path of Pompeius. At present this was unknown to Caesar, although a fresh difficulty was already threatening him. The origin of this was the device of Pompeius in publishing through all the provinces and native states exaggerated and glowing accounts of the late battle before Durazzo, accounts that were wholly unwarranted by the actual facts; the result of which was to propagate a widespread rumor that Caesar had been beaten, and was now in headlong flight with the virtual loss of all his army. In consequence, the roads had been rendered exceedingly hostile, and some of the local townships actually contemplated desertion from the Caesarian cause; and though numerous messengers were dispatched by various routes from Caesar to Domitius and from Domitius to Caesar, they all alike found it impossible to get through. Fortunately the cavalry scouts of Domitius were sighted on the march by the party of Allobroges—those friends of Roucillus and Egus whose treachery we have already recorded: and either through the force of old associations (they having served together in the Gallic wars), or else through swollen vanity, these men now gave their former comrades a full and correct account of what had really taken place, and particularly of Caesar's departure from before Durazzo and the simultaneous advance of Pompeius. This information was at once reported to Domitius; and though he had barely four hours' start, yet, thanks to his friend the enemy, he succeeded in escaping his danger, and at the town of Kalambaka (*Aeginium*), which lies directly across the approach into Thessaly, met Caesar in full career towards him.

The junction of the two Caesarian armies thus safely effected, the advance was continued to Palaea Episkopi (*Gomphi*), the first town of Thessaly as you enter from Epirus. This people had a few months earlier in the war, and quite unsolicited, sent envoys to Caesar, putting all their resources at his free disposal, and asking only for a garrison to be sent down to them. Unluckily the garbled version of the battle at Durazzo, noticed above, had had time to reach the city, and had greatly magnified the importance of that event. The effect was soon apparent. Androsthenes, the chief native magistrate of Thessaly, preferring to range himself on the side of a victorious Pompeius rather than share the misfortunes of a Caesar, required the entire rural population, slave no less than free, to withdraw inside the town, and then closed the gates against all comers. At the same time he sent off urgent messages for help to Scipio and Pompeius, informing them that he had full confidence in the strength of the town defenses if quickly relieved, but that he could not endure any protracted siege. At this particular moment in the course of events Scipio had just heard of the break-up of the armies round Durazzo, and in consequence had marched his legions to Larissa, while Pompeius was still some distance from the Thessalian border. Caesar, therefore, after first fortifying a camp, ordered the construction of scaling-ladders and battery-sheds, and the preparation of defensive hurdles. Then, as soon as these were ready, he appealed to his troops, pointing out to them how much it would conduce to the relief of their general state of want, if they could gain possession of a well-stocked and wealthy town, and by the example they made of it strike terror into the counsels of other communities: above all, if they did this at once, before the reinforcements from outside had time to concentrate. The men answered by an extraordinary display of enthusiasm, and accordingly the assault of the town was taken in hand on the same day as their arrival before it; and though the walls were of great height and it was already past four in the afternoon, yet by sundown the place had been carried and given over as plunder to the troops.[12] Without further delay the camp was then moved from the neighborhood of the town, and the army continued its march to Metropolis,[13] outstripping the tidings and even the rumor of the captured city.

At first the Metropolitans were inclined to adopt the policy of their neighbors, influenced as they were by the same idle stories: a little later, however, on learning the fate that had overtaken the Gomphians from the lips of the prisoners purposely sent up to the wall by Caesar, they threw open their city gates. They were treated with the utmost consideration; and the contrast drawn between the easy lot of the Metropolitans and the ruinous end of Gomphi was so significant, that not a single state in all Thessaly, with the sole exception of Larissa, which was strongly held by Scipio's armies, subsequently refused adhesion to Caesar or compliance with his demands. He, meanwhile, had selected a suitable camping-ground in the open country, where the corn crops were now all but ripe, and resolved to await there the approach of Pompeius, and to make this place decide once for all the issue of the campaign.

As for his opponent, a few days after these operations he crossed the Thessalian frontier, and, in the course of an harangue delivered to his now united army, expressed his thanks to the men of his own command for their past services to himself; and then, turning to the troops under Scipio, asked them to be willing, though the main victory was already won, to accept a share of the spoils and rewards of the campaign. After that, the legions were all concentrated within one camp, and Pompeius, courteously dividing with Scipio his privileges as commander, ordered all bugle-calls to be repeated before that general, and a second headquarters tent to be pitched for him.

Such an increase of numbers on the part of the Pompeians, and the successful junction of their two powerful armies did but confirm the general belief that had long been prevalent amongst them. So certain indeed grew their hopes of victory, that any pause in the conduct of the operations seemed but to delay their own return to Italy, and any movement on the part of Pompeius, that exhibited unusual deliberateness and caution, could always, according to his critics, have been well finished off in a single day; and he was loudly accused of toying with his command, and of treating as menials men who had filled the highest offices in the State.[14] Much controversy also ensued amongst the rival claimants to the various prizes of the war, notably the great public priesthoods, whilst the consulship was settled in advance over a number of years. Others claimed the houses and property of those in the Caesarian camp; and a heated dispute arose in open council on the case of Lucilius Hirrus, at that moment away on a mission from Pompeius to the Parthian court, and on his right to stand in his absence as a candidate at the approaching praetorian elections. Thus while his friends appealed to the plighted word of Pompeius and the obligation incumbent upon him of fulfilling the pledge given at his departure (unless indeed he wished Hirrus to be thought a fool for trusting to his support), the rest stoutly maintained that, where the danger and hardships were alike for all, no one man should be given these exceptional privileges. So too the daily bickerings that passed between Lucius Domitius, Scipio, and Lentulus Spinther, on the subject of Caesar's priestly office,[15] had lately degenerated into open brawling of the most offensive character; Lentulus insisting on the claims of seniority, Domitius boasting of his wide influence and prestige in the capital, Scipio confident in his family connection with Pompeius. Another incident at this time was the public indictment of Lucius Afranius by Acutius Rufus for what he alleged to have been the betrayal of the army in Spain; while Lucius Domitius, not to be behindhand, had a separate proposal of his own to submit to the council. This was that on the conclusion of hostilities all those of senatorial rank who had assisted in fighting for the common cause should be constituted a judicial body, with three votes[16] given to each member: sentence should then be passed individually upon everyone who had either stayed behind in Rome, or, while showing themselves inside the Pompeian lines, had taken no active part in the campaign; one ticket to be cast by those who favored complete acquittal, another where the verdict was capital punishment, and a third by those who imposed a fine. Everybody, in short, was engrossed either with his own political interests, or the money-rewards he hoped to reap for party services, or with the prosecution of his private quarrels. Men's minds were no longer concerned with the indispensable conditions of success, but rather with the best use they could make of their victory.

In the meantime Caesar had not been idle. His supplies were now adequately organized, his troops had recovered their *moral,* and a sufficient interval had elapsed since the two battles of Durazzo: and now, to show the implicit trust he reposed in the temper of his men, he resolved to test the extent to which Pompeius either desired or designed a general engagement. His army accordingly moved out of camp and drew up for action, at first on ground of his own choosing and at some little distance from the Pompeian camp, but, later on, advancing well away from the shelter of their own rampart and bringing their line of battle close up to the hills occupied by the

Pompeians. As a result of these tactics the confidence of the army in its own powers strengthened daily.

Yet Caesar did not feel justified in abandoning the practice lately instituted with regard to the cavalry, and already described above; but finding himself greatly outnumbered in this arm of the service, he formed a corps of young soldiers, lightly equipped, and drawn from legionaries of the front rank specially selected for speed of foot. This body was then instructed to fight with their usual equipment, interspersing themselves among the troopers; and by constant daily practice they soon attained a marked proficiency in this new type of warfare. The advantage gained by this device was that one thousand Caesarian horsemen, having once acquired experience, had no hesitation, even on more or less open ground, in standing the charge of the seven thousand who formed the cavalry of Pompeius; and the large numbers of the latter had little terror for their composite enemy. Indeed it was during these few days that a successful cavalry skirmish took place in which one of the two brother Allobroges, whose desertion to Pompeius we have recorded above, was killed, with certain others of his followers. As for the main force of the Pompeians at this time, it was their daily habit to move down from their camp on the hills, and at the lowest spurs of the mountain to form up in order of battle, in constant expectation, it would seem, that Caesar might somehow or other place himself at a disadvantage. When, therefore, it became evident that no artifice could entice his opponent to an action, Caesar determined that for his part the easiest method for the further prosecution of the war was to break up his present encampment, and in future to keep perpetually on the march: calculating that, by constantly changing his camping-ground and moving about from place to place, he would find it easier to feed his troops, and at the same time have opportunities for fighting on the road; on the other hand, the daily marches would exhaust the endurance of Pompeius' army which was not so habituated to fatigue.

Everything was accordingly ready for the new departure; the signal to march had been given, and the tents taken down and stowed away, when it was suddenly observed that the Pompeian battleline, going beyond its daily practice, had a minute or two before advanced a considerable distance from its entrenchments, thus suggesting the possibility of engaging it upon something like equal terms. On receipt of this intelligence Caesar turned to his colleagues, and though his column was by this time in the actual gateways of the camp, "We must give up our march for the present," he said, "and turn our attention to battle, as has always been our earnest wish. We are all ready for a fight: we shall not again easily find the opportunity." And without further delay he led out his forces fully equipped for action.

The same decision to fight had, as was afterwards discovered, been also taken by Pompeius in deference to the urgent solicitations of his party. Such a resolution on his part had been foreshadowed in the council-meetings of the last few days, when he had assured his colleagues that they might expect to see the rout of the Caesarian army even before the two hostile lines were in contact with each other. Noting the looks of surprise called forth by this statement, he had then continued,

> . . . I am well aware that what I promise sounds almost incredible, but to give you greater confidence for going into action, listen to the plan I have formed for the battle. I have induced our cavalry—and they have pledged themselves to the task— immediately we begin to come to close quarters, to attack the right wing of the Caesarians on its exposed flank, and, by riding round the rear of their line, to drive the enemy before them in all the confusion that such a diversion will cause, before even a single spear can be thrown by ourselves. In this way we shall finish off the war without the slightest risk to the legions, and with scarcely a scratch to any of us: whilst, as you will see, the maneuver presents no sort of difficulty owing to our immense preponderance in cavalry.

He ended by a solemn warning to hold themselves ready for all future emergencies, and now that they had their chance of fighting, as had so often occupied their thoughts, to show the world that in point of efficiency and courage they were not unworthy of its high opinion.

He was followed by Labienus, whose supreme contempt for the forces under Caesar was only equalled by the extravagant eulogy he poured upon the plan of Pompeius. "Do not imagine, Sir," said he,

> . . . that this is the army which conquered Gaul and Germany. I was personally present at all those battles, and am not therefore rashly making statements on a subject I do not fully comprehend. A very small fraction of that army now survives: a large proportion of it is dead and gone, as indeed was inevitable where so much fighting had to be done; numbers were carried off by fever in Italy last autumn, numbers again have scattered to their homes, and numbers have been left behind in charge of continental Europe. Surely you yourselves have heard from your correspondents across the water, whose delicate health obliged them to stay at home, how fresh battalions have been formed at Brindisi (*Brundisium*). What you now see before you are corps that have been repleted from the levies in Northern Italy during the last few years, and many of them come from the colonies beyond the Po (*Padus*); while, even so, the pith and kernel of the men have perished in the two battles before Durazzo.

At the end of this speech he bound himself by an oath not to return to camp except as a victor and urged upon the others to follow his example. His action won the warm approval of Pompeius, who immediately took the same oath, and was followed unhesitatingly by the remainder of the staff. At the close of this scene the council broke up amid the light-hearted confidence of all present: imagination already put victory in their grasp; for where the issues involved were so great, and the speaker so trained a master of war, it was impossible not to suppose that he had fully weighed the import of his words.

CHAPTER FIVE

PHARSALUS AND AFTER

AS THE ARMY OF CAESAR APPROACHED THE LINES OF POMPEIUS the following was found to be his adversary's order of battle. The left wing was formed by the two legions, known respectively as the First and Third, which had been surrendered by Caesar on command of the Senate at the opening of the civil troubles: here too was Pompeius himself. The center was occupied by Scipio with his Syrian corps, while the left was in charge of the legion from Cilicia, supported by the Spanish battalions which, as already recorded, Afranius had brought over to his chief. All these troops constituted in Pompeius' judgment the most reliable portion of his army. The remaining units were distributed between the center and wings, and made up a total strength of 110 battalions, or in round numbers forty-five thousand men.[1] About two thousand of these were reservists, time-expired men who had served in Pompeius' permanent bodyguard on previous campaigns, and had now flocked to the standard of their old commander for the present war: these he had parcelled out along his whole line. There were also seven other battalions distributed as garrisons to the main camp and adjacent outposts. Lastly, as his right was firmly protected by a stream presenting steep and difficult banks, he had massed the whole of his cavalry and light-armed bowmen and slingers in a single dense body outside his left wing.

On his side Caesar had followed his customary dispositions, and had placed the Tenth legion on his right and the Ninth on his left,

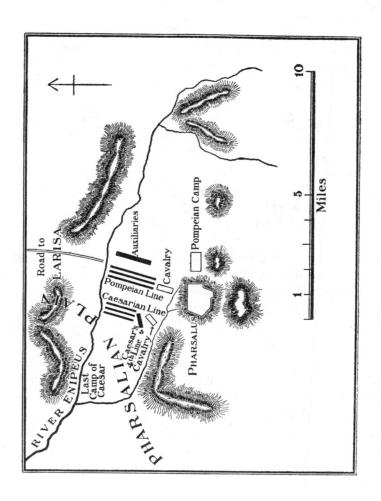

despite the fact that the last-named regiment had suffered so terribly in the battles before Durazzo;[2] it was, however, now coupled with the Eighth, thus forming practically one legion out of two, each of whom had orders to support the other. Eighty battalions altogether had taken their place in the line, amounting to twenty-two thousand troops, while two more had been left behind to hold the camp. Marcus Antonius had been appointed to command the left, Publius Sulla the right, and Cnaeus Domitius the center: Caesar himself took his stand facing Pompeius. But the discovery of the enemy's peculiar distributions as just described had rendered him uneasy as to the safety of his right wing, in case he should find it turned by the overwhelming cavalry opposed to it. At this moment, therefore, he rapidly drafted from his third or rearmost line a single battalion from each of the legions represented in it; these he then formed into a fourth, so placed as to confront the hostile horsemen, with minute instructions as to the part they were to perform, and an intimation that on their personal gallantry depended the fortunes of the day. At the same time both the third line and the whole of the army were warned not to charge without his special orders, but that when the proper moment came he would give the flag-signal to engage.

In addressing his army with the customary exhortations to battle, and in emphasizing the unbroken continuance of his own services to his men, special stress was laid on the fact that he could call them personally to witness how anxiously he had desired to bring about a settlement. He need only recall the verbal negotiations instituted through Vatinius, the mission of Aulus Clodius to Scipio, and the strenuous appeal made at Oricum to Libo with a view to the dispatch of peace envoys. They might rest assured it had never been his object to trifle with the lives of Roman soldiers, nor yet to rob his country of either one or the other of the two great armies which now stood face to face.

At the close of his speech, as his men were clamoring to advance and burning with the excitement of battle, without further delay he gave the signal by trumpet.

Now there was serving in the army of Caesar a certain reservist named Crastinus, a man of magnificent courage, who the year before had been his senior centurion of the Tenth legion. This man, as soon as the signal sounded, exclaimed to those near him, "Follow me, my old comrades, and give your general the support you have agreed to give him. This is the last battle left us: only see this through, and he is restored to his rightful position and we get back our liberty." Then glancing at Caesar, he added, "I'll manage today, General, that dead or alive you shall have cause to thank me." With these words he dashed out from the right wing at the head of the line, and was at once followed by 120 men of the same company, specially picked troops who were serving as volunteers.

Between the two hostile lines there remained only just sufficient space for each army to deliver its charge. Notwithstanding this, Pompeius had issued previous instructions to his men to stand strictly on the defensive in meeting the attack of the Caesarians, so as to allow their advancing line to become disorganized. This order he was said to have given upon the advice of Caius Triarius, under the belief that the opening rush of the enemy's legions would have its force dissipated by their loss of accurate formation, while his own troops, by maintaining their proper distances, could then fall upon the broken ranks of their opponents. He further hoped that the impact of the falling javelins would be less if his men were kept to their positions, than if they were allowed to run in and meet the hail of spears; while the double distance the Caesarians would have to traverse might well be expected to render them breathless with exhaustion.

In our judgment this decision of Pompeius has nothing to recommend it. There is in all men a certain instinctive courage and combativeness implanted in us by Nature, which is only kindled by the excitement of battle. This instinct it should be the object of commanding officers not to repress but to encourage; and there was sound reason in the ancient practice of letting the bugles call the advance over all the field at once, followed by a single shout from all the men: such a custom, it was found, struck terror into the ranks of the enemy no less than it stimulated their own side. In this particular instance our troops, who at the given signal had dashed forward with brandished spears, on finding that the Pompeians were not advancing to meet them, instinctively slackened speed; and, taught by the accumulated experience of past battles, halted some halfway across the open ground, so as not to spend their strength before coming up with their enemy. Here taking a short rest, and then resuming their rush, they discharged their volley of heavy javelins, and in obedience to Caesar's orders instantly drew their broadswords. Nor, to tell the truth, did the Pompeians show any desire to shirk the encounter, but, parrying the flying spears with their shields, they boldly met the shock of the charging legions with unbroken ranks, and, after hurling their own javelins, went to work with the sword. At the same time their cavalry, acting upon its previous instructions, advanced from the left wing in one dense mass, whilst the mob of archers also commenced to spread themselves over the ground. This attack was more than our own cavalry could cope with, and slowly giving way they recoiled before the onslaught. Thereupon the enemy's horsemen, pushing home the assault with still fiercer vigor, began deploying in squadrons preparatory to surrounding our main battleline on its exposed flank. Perceiving the threatened danger, Caesar gave the signal to his fourth line, which he had recently improvised out of a number of disconnected battalions. Advancing at high speed and with colors flying, this force delivered such a furious attack upon the opposing cavalry,[3] that not a single trooper stood against them; but, wheeling in a body, they not only evacuated their position in the line, but galloping on in headlong flight took cover in a range of lofty hills. Their dispersal left the archers and slingers wholly unprotected, and being altogether without defensive armor the whole helpless crowd was slaughtered to a man. Following up this exploit, the same force went on without a halt to surround the Pompeian left, which they found still fighting and maintaining a stubborn resistance in line, when it was thus taken unexpectedly in the rear. It was at this critical moment in the battle that Caesar's third line, which had hitherto remained quietly in position, received its orders to advance. His exhausted troops in front were thus replaced by fresh and vigorous reserves; and assailed as they also were from behind, the resistance of the Pompeians at length gave way, and the whole line broke and fled. But though the victory was won, it did not escape the attention of Caesar that the first steps towards its consummation had been the work of those battalions which he had posted in his fourth line to hold in check the Pompeian horse, precisely as he had indicated in his address to the men. It was they who, in the first place, had effected the rout of the cavalry; it was they, again, who had cut to pieces the slingers and archers: finally, it was they who, by turning the left of the Pompeian line, had started the general flight. In the meanwhile Pompeius, on perceiving the disaster to his mounted troops, and the crippling panic pervading that branch of his army on which he chiefly relied, and despairing of success from other quarters, had withdrawn from the fighting line and galloped rapidly back to camp. There, as he passed the pickets on duty outside the frontal gate, he called in loud tones to the centurions in charge, so that the men might catch his words: "Look to the camp, and in case of accident defend it with care. I am going the round of the other gates in order to encourage the troops on guard."

So saying, he made straight for head quarters: in gloomy anticipation of the verdict of the day, yet waiting to learn the end.

Meanwhile his routed followers had also been driven back to their camp and there forced over the trenches. Caesar strongly felt the desirability of giving no breathing space to the terrified rabble, and urged upon his men to take Fortune while in the mood, and to carry the camp by storm. In spite of the great heat—the affair had been protracted to midday—his troops, whom nothing now could stop, gave willing obedience to their commander's orders. The camp was vigorously defended by the force left behind for that purpose, and still more fiercely by the Thracians and other foreign auxiliaries: as for the fugitives from the battle, they were so demoralized with panic and physically so exhausted, that in most cases their arms and standards were indiscriminately flung away, and they were far more concerned with continuing their flight than with staying to hold the camp. And, indeed, it was but a momentary resistance that could be offered against the deadly discharge of our spears even by the force which had manned the ramparts: compelled by their wounds to relinquish their posts, they quickly followed the lead of their regimental and company officers, and fled precipitately to the heights that adjoined the camp.

Inside the Pompeian lines the eye fell upon the spectacle of arbors artificially constructed, of masses of silver plate laid out for present use, of tents paved with cool, fresh cut sods, and even, in the case of Lentulus and others, protected from the heat by ivy. Many other indications could likewise be discerned of extravagant luxury and of confidence in coming victory, rendering it an easy assumption that men who went so far out of their way in the pursuit of superfluous pleasures could have had no misgivings as to the issue of the day. Yet these were the men who habitually taunted the poverty-stricken, long-suffering army of Caesar with the charge of being voluptuaries; whereas in truth they had all along been in want of the barest necessaries.

But to return to Pompeius. Delaying his departure until our troops were actually in motion within his lines, he seized a horse and, tearing off all outward signs of his marshal's rank, fled through the postern gate, where, putting spurs to his mount, he headed in the direction of Larissa. Making no halt at that town, but maintaining the same rapid rate of traveling, and merely picking up a few followers from the general rout, he continued his journey without intermission through the night; and, with an escort of no more than thirty troopers, at length reached the sea. There he embarked on board a corn-ship, repeatedly complaining, so it was said, that his expectations had been wofully falsified, that the very men in whom he had placed his hopes of victory had been the first to fly, and, to judge by appearances, had virtually betrayed him.

Master of the Pompeian camp, Caesar once more appealed to his troops not to let their natural anxiety for plunder hinder the execution of those measures still necessary for the full realization of their victory. Once more they yielded to his wishes, and preparations were immediately begun for the circumvallation of the high ground to which the enemy had retreated. But as the hill was found to be without water, the Pompeians, distrusting the position, had determined to abandon it and to follow the line of heights in a general retirement towards Larissa. Their intentions were at once detected by Caesar. Dividing his forces, he ordered part of his legions to remain in the captured camp of Pompeius, another division to be sent back to his own camp, while he himself with the remaining four set out on the task of heading off the retreating Pompeians by taking an easier route. At the end of six miles he was in a position to form up in line of battle; whereupon the enemy halted on one of the numerous hills. The base of this hill was washed by a stream; and in order to prevent his opponents from watering during the night, Caesar made one last appeal to his weary troops: and, exhausted as they were by their long day's work, with night already upon them, they nevertheless succeeded in interposing between the hill and the river a fully forti- fied breastwork. On the completion of this work the enemy sent in a deputation to open negotiations for surrender; at the same time a few representatives of the senatorial order who had attached themselves to the mission, took the opportunity to seek personal safety by escap- ing under cover of night.

As soon as it was day, the order was given for the whole party up on the hill to descend from the high ground to the plain below, and there to throw down their arms. This they did without demur, and then, flinging themselves to the earth, with weeping eyes and hands upraised, they begged their lives of Caesar. In reassuring tones he bade them rise, and after a brief reference to his well-known clem- ency in order to appease their fears, granted their lives to all, and then transferred them to the kindly attentions of his own men, with strict injunctions that no one was to be in anyway injured or to lose any of his property. Having thus provided for the care of his prisoners, he immediately ordered up other legions from camp, while those who had come on with him were directed to take their turn of rest and then to rejoin their old quarters. With these arrangements completed, he marched through to Larissa on the same day.

His own casualties from this battle did not exceed two hundred rank and file, though on the other hand he had to deplore the loss of fully thirty centurions—gallant men whom he could ill spare. Among the slain also was the Crastinus mentioned above, killed by a sword- thrust straight in the face, as he fought with desperate courage. His conduct had amply justified the words he uttered on going into battle. In Caesar's judgment the palm of valor in this action belonged to Crastinus: and deep was his sense of gratitude for the man's devotion to himself. Of the Pompeian army some fifteen thousand were esti-mated to have fallen,[4] while the total number of prisoners taken exceeded twenty-four thousand, a number which included the gar-risons of outposts who afterwards surrendered to Sulla, besides large bodies also which sought shelter in the neighboring townships. Of bat-talion and company colors 180 were brought in to Caesar as the total list of trophies from the battle, and nine eagles of distinct legions. Finally it should be mentioned that Lucius Domitius, while endeavor-ing to escape from camp to the hills, was overtaken and cut down by our cavalry, when his strength had now given out through fatigue.

While the issue was thus decided on land, a hostile fleet, this time under the command of Decimus Laelius, had again visited Brindisi. Adopting the same plan of action that Libo, it will be remembered, had attempted before him, he seized as his base the island off the mouth of the harbor; only to be met by a similar scheme of defense on the part of Vatinius, then acting as governor of Brindisi. Having carefully screened and fitted out a number of small boats, Vatinius enticed the ships of Laelius to venture inside; and one of these, a five-decker,[5] having advanced too far, was captured in the narrow entrance to the port together with two other smaller craft. This success he followed up by stationing along the foreshore, just as his predecessor had done before him, a series of cavalry patrols to prevent the hostile fleet from watering. Laelius, however, had the advantage of a better season of the year for purposes of navigation, and bringing up water supplies for his force by merchant boats from Corfu and Durazzo, showed he was not to be lightly deterred from his project: in fact, it was only after the news of the battle fought in Thessaly, that either the ignominious loss of his vessels or his want of necessary stores could induce him to quit his hold upon the island and harbor.

Almost contemporary with this raid was a descent of Caius Cas-sius upon Sicily with his divisional fleet of Syrian, Phoenician, and Cilician squadrons. Caesar's own fleet, it must be explained, had been divided into two separate commands: half of it was stationed at Vibo-on-Straits (*Monteleone*) under the praetor Publius Sulpicius, the other half lay off Messina (*Messana*), under Marcus Pomponius.

Yet in spite of these dispositions, Cassius succeeded in swooping down with his ships upon Messina before any whisper of his coming reached the ears of Pomponius, who was thus caught in a state of great confusion, with no scouting vessels on the lookout and no settled formation in his squadron. The wind was high and favored the design of Cassius. Filling a number of old merchantmen with pine, pitch, tow, and other inflammable materials, he launched them against the Pomponian fleet with such deadly effect that the whole thirty-five vessels, twenty being decked boats, were quickly burned to the water-line. A widespread panic followed upon this exploit, and notwithstanding the presence in Messina of a garrison legion, the town was with difficulty retained for Caesar: indeed, had it not been that at this very moment the first tidings came through of his recent victory on land, conveyed by a chain of mounted patrols, the general opinion was that it would inevitably have been lost. As it was, the fortunate arrival of this news made the defense of the city possible, and Cassius thereupon sailed away to Vibo to turn his attentions to the squadron under Sulpicius. Here, finding our ships to be moored close in to shore, owing to their infection with the same general panic, his crews prepared to repeat their former tactics. Helped by a favorable wind, some forty odd merchantmen were carefully fitted out as fireships, and then sent in among the enemy's fleet; and, the fire taking hold on either wing, five of their number were soon completely gutted. As the flames continued to spread with the force of the gale, the detachment of veterans from Caesar's sick-list who had been left by him in charge of this fleet could no longer endure the insult: without waiting for orders, they manned some of the vessels and, putting out to sea, attacked the fleet of Cassius, capturing two five-deckers (one of which had the admiral on board who only escaped by taking to a boat), and sending two of the three-deckers to the bottom. Soon afterwards there arrived definite intelligence of the battle just fought in Thessaly, so explicit as to convince even the Pompeians, who hitherto had affected to believe that the reports current were merely the inventions of Caesar's officers and friends. With this authentic information Cassius removed his squadron from those waters.

Meanwhile it was clear to Caesar that every other object should be subordinated to the supreme task of pursuing Pompeius into whatever corner of the world his flight might have taken him; on no account must he be allowed to collect fresh forces and so to renew the war. As fast, therefore, as his cavalry could cover the ground, he was now daily pressing hard on his heels, having first left orders for one of the legions to follow by easier stages. A decree had already been published at Amphipolis[6] in the name of Pompeius, commanding the presence of every man of military age in the province, no matter whether Greek or Roman, with the object of being sworn in for active service; but whether he had issued this edict in order to avert suspicion and so conceal to the last moment his plans for a more protracted flight, or whether he contemplated the defense of Macedonia by means of fresh levies in the event of not being immediately pursued, was a question on which there were no satisfactory means of forming an opinion. At any rate what he actually did was to lie off the town at anchor for a single night, and to summon on board his Greek friends, from whom he borrowed money for his personal expenses; and then, on the news of Caesar's approach, set sail from the place and arrived after a few days at Mytilini (*Mytilene*). Here he was delayed two days by bad weather, after which, having been joined by some other fast craft, he continued his voyage to Cilicia, from whence he crossed to Cyprus. At Cyprus he was met by intelligence that the citadel of Antioch had, as the result of a concerted movement on the part of both native inhabitants and the Roman citizens settled there in business, been forcibly occupied with a view to his exclusion from the city; and that an express warning had been dispatched to those refugees from the battle who were reported as having sheltered in towns of the immediate vicinity, that they would do well not to approach Antioch,[7] and that any such step on their part would be taken at their own imminent peril. A similar incident had happened at Rhodes to Lucius Lentulus, consul the preceding year, Publius Lentulus an ex-consul, and to various others. These men had arrived off the island in the course of their flight after Pompeius, only to find themselves refused admission to either town or harbor: an intimation was served upon them that they must quit the neighborhood, and sorely against their will they had been obliged to set sail.

Another cause that helped to determine this attitude of the native populations was the rumor of Caesar's advance, which by this time was circulating amongst them.

Knowledge of these facts induced Pompeius to abandon all design of visiting Syria. He therefore seized the funds of the local revenue company, supplementing these by private loans, and at the same time took on board ship a large sum of copper coinage for war purposes. He then armed a force of two thousand men, partly drawn from the staff of the official revenue officers, partly pressed from the resident mercantile houses, and, incorporating with them such private servants of his own friends as their masters considered fit for the enterprise on hand, with this force he arrived at Pelusium.[8] Here, as chance would have it, he found the Egyptian king, Ptolemy, a mere boy in years, at present engaged at the head of a formidable military force in a war with his sister Cleopatra, whom a few months earlier he had expelled from the kingdom by the help of his kinsmen and supporters; the two camps of brother and sister being only a short distance apart. To him, therefore, Pompeius sent a request that, in consideration of the ties of hospitality and friendship which had existed between himself and the boy's father, he might be allowed to enter Alexandria and to find protection in the monarch's resources during this his hour of adversity. Unfortunately his envoys, after discharging the duties of their mission, entered into conversation, in rather too unguarded terms, with the royal troops, pressing them to take up the cause of their leader, and not to look askance upon his present humble circumstances. Of these troops the greater part were old soldiers of Pompeius, whom Gabinius had taken over from Pompeius' army of the East when succeeding to the governorship of Syria, and subsequently had brought across to Alexandria; where, at the close of the war for which they were imported, they had been left behind in the service of Ptolemy, the father of the present boy.

The discovery of these advances on the part of the officers by the king's advisers, who, owing to his minority, were then administering the kingdom, determined them at once to take action. It may be they were filled with a genuine alarm (so at least they afterwards declared), that the tampering with the royal army might lead to a military occupation of Alexandria and Egypt by Pompeius; or—since misfortune usually converts friends to foes—they may have thought it safe to show contempt for fallen greatness; at all events they first gave a favorable answer in public to Pompeius' envoys, bidding him come to the king, and then, secretly conspiring amongst themselves, dispatched a certain fellow named Achillas, the holder of a command in the royal household and a desperado of singular boldness, together with Lucius Septimius, an officer of regimental rank, with directions to murder Pompeius. These two approached their chief victim with greetings of marked cordiality; and, as he already possessed some slight acquaintance with Septimius, who had served under him as a company officer[9] in the war with the pirates, he was induced to go on board their mere cockleshell of a boat along with a few members of his suite. There he was foully murdered by Achillas and Septimius; and with like treachery Lucius Lentulus was arrested under the king's orders, and was put to death in his dungeons.

To continue now the narrative of Caesar's movements. On arrival in Asia Minor he found that an attempt had been made by Titus Ampius to remove from Ephesus the treasures in the temple of Diana. For this purpose all the Roman senators in the province had been summoned to certify to the amount of specie taken; but his own rapid approach had disturbed the proceedings, and Ampius had in the meanwhile taken to flight. Thus for the second time Caesar was instrumental in saving the treasures of the Ephesian goddess. Equally significant was the well-attested fact that in the temple of Minerva at Elis,[10] on the very day of his successful battle, as was found by a careful calculation of the dates, the statue of Victory, whose place in the temple was in front of Minerva herself and which had hitherto faced the statue of that deity, turned itself round to the temple doors with its face towards the entrance. Again, at Antioch in Syria, twice on the same day there was heard the shout of an army advancing into battle, and so clear a blast of trumpets that the whole body of citizens rushed in full armor to their places on the walls. The same portent was repeated at Ptolemais;[11] while at Bergama (*Pergamum*) in the inmost recesses of the temples, where none but the priests are allowed to enter and which the Greeks call "sanctuaries,"[12] the noise of cymbals was distinctly heard: and at Tralles[13] in the temple of Victory, where a bust of Caesar had been lately consecrated, a palm tree was pointed out as having during those days sprouted through the masonry of the roof, between the joints of the stonework.

It was while still in Asia Minor, after a halt of a few days, that intelligence reached Caesar that Pompeius had been seen in Cyprus, leading to the obvious conjecture that Egypt was his goal; not merely on the ground of his own intimate connection with that kingdom, but also because of the other signal advantages offered by its position. He accordingly embarked with the single legion that he had ordered to follow from Thessaly, and a second which had been detached from Greece (*Achaia*) from the command of Quintus Fufius; and with the addition of eight hundred horse and ten Rhodian men-of-war and a few others from Asiatic ports, crossed the sea to Alexandria. Of these two legions the present strength was only three thousand two hundred men: the remainder of the corps had been unable to reach him, some disabled by wounds received in battle, others by the exhaustion following on their long and fatiguing march. Yet even with such weak supports he had not hesitated to continue his advance; and relying on the moral effect produced by the report of his recent victory he concluded that all places would prove equally safe for him. At Alexandria he heard of the death of Pompeius; and he had no sooner set foot on shore, than he was greeted by a shout of challenge from the troops whom the king had left to garrison the city, and a crowd was seen coming out to protest against the official insignia[14] which were carried before him. Such a display, the whole mob declared, was a slight upon the royal dignity.

This disturbance was successfully quelled; but subsequently, owing to the turbulence of the populace, frequent riots became of daily occurrence, and in every quarter of the city numbers of our troops were killed. Seeing therefore the threatening aspect of the situation, Caesar sent orders to Asia Minor for a further reinforcement, namely, the legions which had quite recently been embodied from the surrendered Pompeian infantry: it was impossible for him now to draw back, since his own force was effectively cooped up in Alexandria by the Etesian winds which so seriously impede navigation from that port.

Pending their arrival, he determined to investigate the dispute between the two sovereigns of the country. Such a task he regarded as falling distinctly within the sphere of Roman interests, and of his own activities as chief magistrate;[15] while the circumstance that it was in his first consulship that a treaty of alliance, ratified by both Senate and popular assembly, had been negotiated with their father Ptolemy, constituted a special claim upon his own good offices. He therefore announced his decision that King Ptolemaeus and his sister Cleopatra should each disband the armies they had on foot, and fight out their dispute by process of law before himself rather than by an appeal to arms between each other. At that time the regent in charge of the kingdom during the boy's minority was a certain eunuch named Pothinus. This fellow now began to protest indignantly, amongst his own adherents, against the notion of a king being summoned to trial; and having after a while won over some of the king's advisers to the support of his scheme, he secretly sent an order calling up the native army from Pelusium to Alexandria, and appointing to the supreme command the Achillas whom we have already mentioned. In a written dispatch, supplemented by a verbal message, he first excited the ambition of the newly promoted generalissimo by private promises of his own, further enforced by those of the king, and then proceeded to give him minute instructions as to the steps he was to take.

Meanwhile Caesar found that in the will of the late king Ptolemy there were set down as joint heirs the senior of his two sons and the elder of his two daughters; and to secure this settlement he had added an earnest appeal to Rome, by all that was sacred and by the treaties negotiated with us in the capital, that these dispositions should not be disturbed. One copy of this instrument had been brought to Rome by special envoys of the king, to be deposited in the Treasury (though owing to the press of public business this had not been carried out, the document being stored for safety at the residence of Pompeius), while a duplicate version fully signed had been left for future reference at Alexandria. The whole matter was under investigation by Caesar, whose sole desire was to effect a settlement between the two rulers in the character of a common friend and arbitrator, when the proceedings were suddenly interrupted by the startling announcement that the royal army with all its cavalry was marching on Alexandria. In this emergency Caesar, whose forces were by no means so numerous that he could safely rely on them if compelled to fight outside the walls, had no alternative but to confine himself to his own quarter inside the city, and there to ascertain the intentions of Achillas. At the same time his troops all received orders to remain under arms, and the king was strongly urged to send a deputation to Achillas from among his own most trusted advisers, to convey to him his pleasure in the matter. Two of these were accordingly dispatched, viz. Dioscorides and Serapion, both of them men who had visited Rome as plenipotentiaries under the elder Ptolemy, in whose counsels they had exercised very considerable influence. These made their way to the Alexandrine, but had no sooner entered his presence than, without either granting them audience or even ascertaining the object of their mission, he gave the word to have them seized and put to death. Thereupon one of the two was savagely wounded and carried off for dead by the intervention of his attendants; the other was murdered outright. This outrage determined Caesar to keep the young king in his own custody; for not only was great weight attached, as he conceived, by the populace to the royal title, but the responsibility for the war would thus be made to appear the independent action of a band of cutthroats rather than the settled determination of the sovereign.

With regard to the forces at the command of Achillas, neither their number, composition, nor experience rendered it safe to hold them in contempt. Fully twenty thousand men were at his disposal. Of these the backbone consisted of the old Gabinian troops, men who by long residence had virtually become naturalized Alexandrines, familiar with all the wild licence characteristic of that city: the pride of race and disciplined habits of Rome had been gradually unlearned: they had married native women, and many of them had children by these alliances. Their ranks were swelled by the sweepings of all the buccaneers and highwaymen that infest Syria, the province of Cilicia, and the neighboring lands, while many a convict whose death sentence compelled him to fly his own country had foregathered in this city. Besides these there was a contingent of our own runaway slaves, who could always count on a safe asylum and an assured means of livelihood in Alexandria, seeing they had only to give in their names to be at once enrolled as soldiers. Should any of their number be afterwards seized by his lawful owner, there was a permanent understanding among the troops that he must at once be rescued, and any hand laid upon one of their fellows would be resisted by them as though their own personal safety were threatened; for they well knew that one and all were involved in a similar delinquency. This was the crew whose custom it was to demand the lives of kings' ministers, to carve up the property of wealthy burgesses, to besiege the royal palace with demands for increased pay, to banish and recall from banishment at their own sweet will; all in obedience to what seems an immemorial tradition for an Alexandrine army. Finally, there was the cavalry, two thousand strong. All these were old campaigners: they had served in the innumerable wars of Alexandria, they had restored Ptolemy to his throne, slain two sons of Bibulus, and fought the native Egyptians—beyond doubt a formidable record.

Relying on this material, with a corresponding contempt for the weak numbers of his enemy, Achillas now took permanent occupation of the whole of Alexandria, except the portion commanded by Caesar and his troops. His first move was an attempt to rush the buildings in which Caesar himself was quartered; but picquets were posted along the streets and the attack was successfully met. Simultaneously, fighting took place down by the harbor, and here by far the most desperate struggle was occasioned. The enemy, dividing his forces, gave battle in several thoroughfares at once, and endeavored by sheer weight of numbers to gain possession of the warships that were lying there. Of these ships fifty formed the fleet that had been recently sent to the support of Pompeius, and after the crushing defeat in Thessaly had since returned home: they were all either four- or five-deckers,[16] and constituted a thoroughly equipped and sea-going force. In addition, there were the twenty-two regular guardships of Alexandria, decked boats everyone. Should, therefore, the enemy once succeed in seizing this formidable flotilla, they would be able to wrench from Caesar his own small squadron, and by their undisputed mastery of the sea cut his communications with the outside world, including all possibility of supplies or reinforcements. The action was therefore contested with all the obstinacy demanded by the crisis; for while with one party success meant a speedy triumph for their arms, defeat for the other meant disaster. Victory, however, rested with Caesar, who, recognizing his inability with so weak a force to control so wide an area, first set fire to the whole fleet and the rest of the ships in the naval yards, and then hastily landed troops close up to Pharus.

Pharus is a lighthouse standing upon the island from which it has taken its name, of immense height, and built on a strikingly massive scale. It is the position of this island opposite Alexandria that forms the harbor of that city, although at its upper part it is connected with the main town by a sea-mole some three-quarters of a mile in length, crowned with a narrow causeway and bridge. It is covered with houses of the native Egyptians, forming a quarter equal in point of size to an ordinary town; and if any passing ships find themselves a trifle out of their course, either through losing their bearings or from stress of weather, they are plundered by its inhabitants quite after the manner of professional pirates. Owing moreover to the narrowness of the passage, the possession of Pharus absolutely controls the entrance to the harbor; and it was the apprehensions excited by this circumstance that now led Caesar, while the enemy's attention was engrossed by the battle, to land troops, occupy the tower, and establish a garrison. He thus secured a safe transit for his oversea supplies and reinforcements, which were now summoned by express orders from all the nearest provinces of the Empire.

In other quarters of the town the day's fighting ended in a drawn battle without the definite repulse of either party, a result due to the restricted nature of the ground; and both sides having sustained slight casualties, Caesar drew a cordon round all the positions of highest strategical value, and on them proceeded under cover of night to construct a line of defense-works. The quarter so enclosed contained a tiny wing of the royal palace where apartments had been found for Caesar upon his first arrival, and also a theater abutting on the palace which served as a citadel, and commanded approaches both to the harbor and the other naval dépôts. These fortifications were then extended on succeeding days until they practically formed a curtain-wall effectually protecting him from being forced to fight against his will.

In the midst of these proceedings the younger daughter of the late king Ptolemy, in the fond hope that the throne was now without an occupant, left her quarters in the palace to join the camp of Achillas, where she at once began to cooperate with him in the conduct of the war. But a quarrel quickly broke out between them on the question of precedence, and this diversion proved greatly to the profit of the common soldiery, as both parties staked heavily to win their good opinion. Meanwhile, the enemy being thus employed, Pothinus, the king's guardian and regent of the kingdom, although professedly acting in the interests of Caesar, was all along busily intriguing by means of secret correspondence with Achillas, whom he exhorted not to lose courage but to go on and persevere with their enterprise. His agents were, however, betrayed and arrested, and he himself thereupon put to death by the orders of Caesar.

Such were the circumstances that occasioned the subsequent Alexandrine war.

ENDNOTES

BOOK I

CHAPTER I

[1] Approximate only, owing to the state of the calendar, which was some five weeks ahead of the season. Any month and day given must be corrected accordingly. Thus Jan. 1, 49 becomes about Nov. 24, 50.

[2] Father-in-law of Pompeius since 52.

[3] As holding full military command Pompeius could not, without forfeiting it, enter the ancient city boundary.

[4] The two Spains, then governed by his deputies. See Introd.

[5] Apparently on the ground that the proceedings involved the appointment to consular provinces, which was exempt from the veto.

[6] A quinquennial office, lately fallen into abeyance. The two censors, when appointed, held the census, revised the senatorial register, and supervised Public Works.

[7] Eight annual magistrates representing the Roman Bench, who could however command troops.

[8] In 59 after Caesar's consulship Pompeius had married his daughter Julia who died in childbirth in 54.

[9] Of *Numidia* (Algeria). See p. 76.

[10] i.e., W. of the Rhine.

[11] Thereby crossing the Rubicon, the small stream that then separated Italy from the Cisalpine Province. "We can still go back," are the words attributed to him by later writers, "but once cross this little bridge, and then the sword must settle everything." Suet. 31.

[12] See Introd.

[13] Containing a special war reserve, originally designed to meet a Gallic invasion.

[14] One of Caesar's laws, 59.

[15] The distinguished general who had deserted Caesar. See Introd.

[16] Pentima on the upper Pescara is only approximately the site of the ancient Corfinium.

[17] The Abruzzi.

[18] The Aterno or Pescara.

[19] Roughly Styria and Carinthia.

[20] One of the great religious corporations.

[21] According to Cicero.

CHAPTER II

[1] Caesar summed up the military situation by remarking that "he went to an army without a general, and should return to a general without an army." Suet. 35.

[2] In Tunis, not far from Bizerta. See Map, following p. 78.

[3] Brindisi, Taranto, and Otranto (Cicero and Appian).

[4] Cicero.

[5] 52 BC Introd.

[6] Modern France.

[7] Neighborhood of Nismes and Ardeche.

[8] East of Arles.

[9] Now the Puig Bordel.

[10] i.e., the right; the shield protecting the left.

[11] i.e., maniple. Introd.

CHAPTER III

[1] See Map, following p. 64.

CHAPTER IV

[1] Introd.

[2] According to an ancient almanac.

[3] Then the boundary between Italy and Gaul.

BOOK II

CHAPTER I

[1] e.g., Notre Dame de la Garde. See Plan.

[2] Only an analogy. The question whether an ancient trireme had three superimposed banks of oars, or one bank with three men to each oar, or even some other formation, is still *sub judice*.

[3] "With suppliant fillets."

[4] A Roman soldier's shield was kept, when not in use, in a leather casing.

CHAPTER II

[1] who had been Governor's Paymaster and Governor of it. See Introd.
[2] One of those who vetoed the Senate's declaration of war. Cf. p. 3.
[3] i.e., from Roman citizens born and bred in the province, like some Anglo-Indians.

CHAPTER III

[1] A decked trireme. See note 2, Bk. II, ch. 1, p. 180.
[2] Used by the great Scipio Africanus at the close of the second Punic War, 204.
[3] A regular custom under the Republic after an adequate victory. Under the Empire the emperor alone held the title. For other instances see p. 117 and p. 144.
[4] From the Abruzzi.
[5] Much of this chapter is slightly conjectural, owing to faulty text.
[6] Not only strategically, but also as the granaries of Italy.
[7] "The axes of his lictors."
[8] On the Adriatic, south of the Pescara. See p. 16.
[9] Neighbors to the Marrucinians on the upper Pescara.
[10] i.e., without the loudly-repeated word of command that was usual.

BOOK III

CHAPTER I

[1] By a law of 342, confirmed by Sulla in 81, ten years must elapse between two tenures of the same magistracy. Caesar had been consul 59. Like many others this law was often broken towards the close of the Republic. Pompeius had been consul in 70, 55, and 52. It was in this last year that the trials mentioned below occurred.
[2] The oldest religious celebration of the united Latin race, held annually on the Alban Mount, under the presidency of Rome. Its date was fixed as early in each civil year as possible, since it was regarded as a sacred confirmation of the powers of the new consuls.
[3] Followed, adds Appian, by the crowds, who begged him to come to terms with Pompeius.
[4] Six hundred, according to Appian, of which one hundred had fighting crews of Romans. According to Cicero, Pompeius' original plan, when driven from Italy, was to take to his "wooden walls" like the Greeks at Salamis.
[5] Brother of Marcus, had lost a Caesarian force during the past year at Veglia in the Adriatic. See p. 154 and p. 143.
[6] Appointed Governor by the Senate, p. 6.

[7] Gabinius, when Governor of Syria in 55, had restored Ptolemy Auletes with a Roman force. See p. 174.

[8] Thus repeating his surprise of Jan. 49. The Pompeians, we read, never dreamed of his crossing in mid-winter, but expected him to wait for the New Year ceremonies at Rome, corresponding to our opening of Parliament.

[9] Now Paleo-Kastro at the south end of the bay of Avlona.

[10] Apparently a lacuna here in MSS which contained the disaster to Antonius and Dolabella at Veglia late in the preceding year.

[11] Close by the future Spalato.

[12] In ancient ordnance the driving force was obtained by suddenly relaxing the tension of strongly-twisted ropes. For these ropes women's hair formed the very best material (*Vitruvius* x. 16. 2).

[13] The genuineness of this last sentence, though found in all MSS, is doubted by most editors.

[14] The hill country near the modern Lake Ochrida. Through it passed the great military trunk road connecting Durazzo with Saloniki (Via Egnatia), the East with the West.

[15] The Pompeian head quarters during forty-nine had been Saloniki (*Thessalonica*), where the exiled senate continued to meet.

[16] Lit. "skins," of which Roman tents were made.

[17] Sixty-five and sixty-two. The aediles had chiefly police duties, the care of markets, aqueducts, distribution of corn, arrangement of the great public games, &c.

[18] Alluding to two of Pompeius' earlier wars. See Introd.

CHAPTER II

[1] An elevated platform for speakers. Cf. The French Tribune.

[2] "Military standards."

CHAPTER III

[1] See Plan, following p. 19.

[2] Triremes.

[3] Quadriremes.

[4] i.e., oarsmen.

[5] Ancient authorities record the story that Caesar in desperation at the delay, tried to cross the Adriatic in a small boat, but was driven back by the boisterous weather. He rallied the frightened sailors by the now proverbial words, "You carry Caesar and his fortunes."

[6] Cf. p. 87.

[7] "Publicans."

[8] "Lictors."

[9] Not far from Missolonghi.

[10] "Biremes."

[11] Two critical positions in the Gallic wars, 52.

[12] I conjecture "ab oleribus" for the unintelligible "a Valeribus" of the MSS Cf. Plin. *N.H.* 19. 21.

[13] Pompeius, on seeing these loaves, is said to have ordered their instant removal through fear of their effect on his own men. "We have to do with wild beasts" was his shuddering comment. Suet. 68.

[14] Conjectural. A considerable gap here in the MSS probably contained Caesar's unsuccessful attempt on Durazzo and Pompeius' counter-attack on Caesar's lines, the narrative of which is now continued.

[15] Centurions.

[16] The Caesarian officers were able to raise a body of Aetolian and Acarnanian auxiliaries who fought at Pharsalus. App. 2. 70.

CHAPTER IV

[1] Probably in the lost section.

[2] See plan.

[3] Centurions.

[4] Caesar is said to have remarked that, had the enemy possessed a general who knew how to conquer, that day would have ended the war. Suet. 36; Appian, *B. C.* 2. 62.

[5] i.e., on the axes of his lictors.

[6] 52, just before the great victory of Alesia.

[7] Here probably occurred the incident recorded by Polyaenus (viii. 13). At one point of the retreat Caesar had a swamp on his left, the sea on his right, and the enemy on his rear. The Pompeian fleet was also "shelling" his troops with missiles of all kinds, when he hit on the simple device of ordering them to transfer their shields from the left to the right side.

[8] Afranius especially urged Pompeius to turn the tables on Caesar by first recovering the West and then leading it against the East, meanwhile holding Caesar in check with the fleet. It was the isolation of Scipio's force and his own fear of losing caste with the Orient that turned the scale the other way. Appian, 2. 65.

[9] Following the course of the Voyussa (*Aous*) and entering Thessaly by the Metsovo Pass—still the high road to Constantinople.

[10] The great military road (*Via Egnatia*).

[11] On the Via Egnatia, distant, according to the ancient Itineraries, some seventy miles from the stage marked "In Candavia."

[12] Ancient authorities agree that Caesar's hungry troops here got considerably out of hand, and that much excess ensued.

[13] Now represented by a village with the generic name Paleo-Kastro.

[14] i.e., as consuls and praetors. They dubbed him "Agamemnon, king of kings." Appian, 2. 67.

[15] Caesar had been Chief Pontiff (Pontifex Maximus) since 63.

[16] "Wax tablets."

CHAPTER V

[1] i.e., regulars. An enormous number of Oriental auxiliaries was also on the ground, though the battle was decided solely by the Italian troops.

[2] This is the legion which had the stiff fight outside Lerida (1. 31), which was greatly endangered during the circumvallation of Durazzo (3. 128) and severely mauled at the final sortie of Pompeius and the subsequent defeat of Caesar (3. 139–43). In the autumn of 49, on returning from Spain, it had headed a serious mutiny at Piacenza (*Placentia*), of which temporary lapse in its loyalty Caesar characteristically says nothing.

[3] Their orders were to keep their heavy javelins (*pila*) and use them to strike at the faces of the mounted men. Plutarch.

[4] According to a Caesarian officer present, only six thousand Italians were killed. If fifteen thousand Romans really fell, it is a striking proof of Caesar's trustworthiness, when the temptation to minimize the slaughter must have been strong. Though Caesar, modestly perhaps, does not mention it, Appian says that both before the battle and at the moment of victory strict orders were given to spare fellow countrymen. "They would have it so"; is said by one of his own officers to have been Caesar's comment as he surveyed the stricken field, "after all my great services, they would have condemned me in their courts, had I not appealed to my army." Suet. 30.

[5] Quinquereme. See note on Trireme, Bk. II, ch. 1, p. 190.

[6] On the Struma or Karasú, one of the chief cities of S. Macedonia.

[7] Capital of Syria.

[8] At the most eastern mouth of the Nile, twenty miles east of Port Said.

[9] Centurion.

[10] In the western Peloponnese about twenty-five miles northwest of Olympia.

[11] Probably Acre in Palestine.

[12] ἄδυτα, "the unapproachable."

[13] In Asia Minor on the Menderez (*Maeander*), now Aidin-Gazelhissar.

[14] The fasces.

[15] Consul.

[16] *Quadriremes or quinqueremes.*

INDEX OF PROPER NAMES

SUGGESTED READING

BRUNT, PETER A. *The Fall of the Roman Republic, and Related Essays.* Oxford: Clarendon Press, 1988.

CAESAR, JULIUS. *Alexandrian War. African War. Spanish War.* Trans. A. G. Way. Cambridge, MA: Harvard University Press, 1955.

————. *The Conquest of Gaul.* Trans. H. J. Edwards. New York: Barnes & Noble, 2005.

CICERO. *Brutus; Orator.* Trans. G. L. Hendrickson and H. M. Hubbell. Cambridge, MA: Harvard University Press, 1939.

————. *Letters to Atticus,* 4 volumes. Trans. D. R. Shackleton Bailey. Cambridge, MA: Harvard University Press, 1999.

————. *Letters to Friends,* 3 volumes. Trans. D. R. Shackleton Bailey. Cambridge, MA: Harvard University Press, 2001.

CRAWFORD, MICHAEL H. *The Roman Republic* (second edition). London: Fontana Press, 1992.

CROOK, JOHN A., Andrew Lintott, and Elizabeth Rawson, Eds. *The Cambridge Ancient History (Second Edition). Volume IX. The Last Age of the Roman Republic, 146–43 BC.* Cambridge: Cambridge University Press, 1994.

EVERITT, ANTHONY. *Cicero: A Turbulent Life.* London: John Murray, 2001.

FLOWER, HARRIET I., ED. *The Cambridge Companion to the Roman Republic.* Cambridge: Cambridge University Press, 2004.

GELZER, MATTHIAS. *Caesar: Politician and Statesman.* Trans. P. Needham. Oxford: Basil Blackwell, 1968.

GRUEN, ERICH S. *The Last Generation of the Roman Republic.* Berkeley: University of California Press, 1995.

HARRIS, WILLIAM V. *War and Imperialism in Republican Rome, 327–70 BC.* Oxford: Oxford University Press, 1979.

HOLLAND, TOM. *Rubicon: The Triumph and Tragedy of the Roman Republic.* New York: Doubleday, 2004.

LUCAN. *The Civil War (Pharsalia).* Trans. J. D. Duff. Cambridge, MA: Harvard University Press, 1928.

MEIER, CHRISTIAN. *Caesar.* Trans. D. McLintock. London: Harper Collins, 1995.

MILLAR, FERGUS. *The Crowd in Rome in the Late Republic.* Ann Arbor: The University of Michigan Press, 2002.

PLUTARCH. *Parallel Lives, VII, Demosthenes and Cicero. Alexander and Caesar.* Trans. B. Perrin. Cambridge, MA: Harvard University Press, 1919.

RAAFLAUB, KURT A., AND MARK TOHER. *Between Republic and Empire: Interpretations of Augustus and his Principate.* Berkeley: University of California Press, 1990.

SEAGER, ROBIN. *Pompey the Great.* Oxford: Blackwell Publishers, 2002.

SUETONIUS. *The Lives of the Caesars.* Trans. J. C. Rolfe. New York: Barnes & Noble, 2004.

SYME, RONALD. *The Roman Revolution.* Oxford: Clarendon Press, 1939.

TAYLOR, LILY ROSS. *Party Politics in the Age of Caesar.* Berkeley: University of California Press, 1949.

YAVETZ, ZWI. *Julius Caesar and His Public Image.* London: Thames and Hudson, 1983.